Per Eidsvig was born in Ålesund, Norway, in 1941. He was educated technical physicist at the Norwegian Institute of Technology (NTH) from 1961 to 1966 and earned an MSc degree. Per has worked in ore prospecting and construction of instruments for the Geological Survey of Norway from 1967 to 1984. He was involved in seismic processing for Geco Prakla from 1985 to 1997 and for Read Well Services from 1997 to 2013. Per was a lecturer in electronics at Stavanger Technical School from 1987 to 1990.

Rune Lødeng was born in Moss, Norway, in 1959. He received his technological education in industrial chemistry at the Norwegian Institute of Technology (NTH) in Trondheim from 1980 to 1984, earned a MSc degree and a PhD from 1988 to 1991. Rune has over 40 years of experience in research within chemistry, catalysis and energy-relevant industrial processing.

The book is dedicated to nature, which deserves to be taken out from the illusions of sustainability and into a professionally scientific solid framework.

Per Eidsvig and Rune Lødeng

ELECTRIFICATION TODAY INCREASES THE CO2 EMISSIONS

HYDROGEN INCREASES THE PROBLEM, ONLY MODERN NUCLEAR POWER MAY SOLVE IT

AUSTIN MACAULEY PUBLISHERS
LONDON * CAMBRIDGE * NEW YORK * SHARJAH

Copyright © Per Eidsvig and Rune Lødeng 2025

The right of Per Eidsvig and Rune Lødeng to be identified as authors of this work has been asserted by them in accordance with sections 77 and 78 of the Copyright, Designs and Patents Act 1988.

All rights reserved. No part of this publication may be reproduced, stored in a retrieval system, or transmitted in any form or by any means, electronic, mechanical, photocopying, recording, or otherwise, without the prior permission of the publishers.

Any person who commits any unauthorised act in relation to this publication may be liable to criminal prosecution and civil claims for damages.

A CIP catalogue record for this title is available from the British Library.

ISBN 9781035879717 (Paperback)
ISBN 9781035879724 (ePub e-book)

www.austinmacauley.com

First Published 2025
Austin Macauley Publishers Ltd®
1 Canada Square
Canary Wharf
London
E14 5AA

We thank everyone who helped us. In special, we gratefully thank Heidi Korkeamäki, our talented Finnish friend, who in a short time has greatly improved the logic in the narrative and also transformed our 'Google translate' into good English.

We also thank a group of about 25 people who are highly skilled in different professions for the good and thorough discussions on the internet on most of the issues concerned in this book.

Spring 2024, somewhere in Norway.

Per & Rune.

Table of Contents

Foreword   15

Last-Power (The Core of the Problem)   18

   Phases into the Future   19

Summary   22

1. A Little About the Authors   25

   1.1 Per   25

   1.2 Rune   27

   1.3 Roy   28

2. A Formula for CO2 Emissions, And We Will Write a Book   30

   2.1 We Find a Formula for CO2 Emissions   30

   2.2 Example: CO2 Emission from an Electric Car and a Fossil Car   32

      2.2.1. The energy chain for drift of the electric car   33

      2.2.2. The energy chain for drift of the fossil car   35

      2.2.3. Comparison between CO2 emission from equally heavy electric and fossil cars   36

      2.2.4. What happens when gas power becomes Last-power?   36

      2.2.5. The formula is generally valid   37

      2.2.6. Manufacture of batteries for electric cars   38

   2.3. About the Formula for the CO2 Consequence of Last-power   38

   2.4. It Had to be a Book   40

Summary Chapter 2   *41*

3. Emissions, Electrification And Some More   42

3.1. Data for Power Generation and CO2 Emissions   *42*

3.2. Energy Density   *44*

3.3. Last-power   *45*

    3.3.1. All other power sources are used to the maximum   47

    3.3.2. But Norway does not have coal power!   48

3.4. Infill-power   *49*

    3.4.1. Pump power   49

    3.4.2. Battery power   50

    3.4.3. Concluding comment   51

    3.4.4. Thermodynamics principles   51

3.5. How to Minimise CO2 Emissions   *53*

    3.5.1. Simple justification for electrification today being powered by coal power   53

    3.5.2. About number of steps and efficiency   54

    3.5.3. The time of the fairy tales   55

3.6. Hydrogen, H2   *55*

    3.6.1. H2: Chemistry, colours and energy conditions   56

    3.6.2. The carbon footprint of the Last-power   57

    3.6.3. Niche possibilities for green hydrogen   58

    3.6.4. Use of "surplus power" to produce H2   59

    3.6.5. A small Molboar story from our close reality   59

    3.6.6. Scale considerations   61

        3.6.6.1. EUs headless plans   61

        3.6.6.2. Consequences of H2 export and efficiency   62

    3.6.7. Hydrogen as a greenhouse gas   65

    3.6.8. A small story about today's sad Norwegian hydrogen illusion   65

3.7. E-fuels (Liquid Hydrocarbon) and Ammonia   *66*

    3.7.1. About power production, emerging alternatives   67

    3.7.2. Toxic fuel on the tank   72

    3.7.3. E-Ammonia production from an energy perspective   73

    3.7.4. Other energy losses in production of NH3 used as a H2 carrier for fuel cell applications   75

    3.7.5. Possibilities with the oxyfuel method   75

3.8. Biofuels   *78*

    3.8.1. Introduction   78

    3.8.2. Perspectives and scope   78

3.9. Summary of Green H2, E-fuels, and Bio   *80*

Summary Chapter 3   *81*

4. Time Perspectives   83

4.1. Future Increased Power Demand   *83*

4.2. Reductions in CO2 Emissions Require the Right Action at the Right Time   *85*

4.3. The Extent of the Change We are Going Through   *86*

4.4. The Gaps in Society's Strategy   *94*

4.5. Reduced Standard of Life, but Better Standard of Living?   *95*

Summary Chapter 4   *96*

5. About Realism and Feasibility   98

5.1. The Challenges Quantified in the Big Picture   *98*

    5.1.1. Random and unrealistic objectives   98

    5.1.2. Global perspective   98

5.2. CCS on a Large Scale   *100*

    5.2.1. Introduction   100

5.2.2. What is the status now?	101
5.2.3. Maturity of the technology	102
5.2.4. The Realism of CCS	103
5.2.5. Can CCS be used for anything?	104
5.2.6. CCS and HSE	105
5.2.6.1. Chemicals and environment	105
5.2.6.2. The eternal perspective and CO2 leaks	106
5.2.7. Other barriers and limitations to CCS	106
5.2.8. Capture of CO2 directly from the air?	107
5.3. Illusory and Real Power	*108*
5.3.1. Earmarking	108
5.3.2. The residual energy mix and carbon footprint	109
5.3.2.1. Power properties for sale	109
5.3.2.2. The primary cause of carbon footprint	110
5.3.2.3. Emissions from direct electrified transport	111
5.3.2.4. Emissions from e-hydrogen	113
Summary Chapter 5	*113*
6. Nuclear Power	**116**
6.1. The Need for Nuclear Power	*116*
6.2. Types of Nuclear Power	*118*
6.2.1. Fusion nuclear power	118
6.2.2. 2nd and 3rd generation fission nuclear power	119
6.2.3. 4th-generation nuclear power, 4GNP	119
Safety:	120
Fuel:	121
Economy:	121
Application potential:	121

    Time perspective: 122

6.3 A Plan for Implementation of 4GNP   *122*

Summary Chapter 6   *123*

7. Weaknesses of CO2 Taxes And Climate Quotas   **125**

7.1. National CO2 Taxes   *125*

7.2. CO2 Border Taxes   *126*

7.3. Climate Quotas   *126*

    7.3.1. But surely the climate quotas solve all the problems?   *126*

    7.3.2. Have we become too many?   *131*

Summary Chapter 7   *132*

8. Social Psychology   **133**

8.1. What is an Illusion?   *133*

8.2. We Don't Know What We Don't Know   *134*

8.3. A Bit About Illusions and What We Would Like to Believe   *135*

    8.3.1. How do illusions arise?   *135*

    8.3.2. How illusions control our thought processes   *137*

8.4. On Electrification and Prevailing Illusions   *138*

8.5. Examples of Illusions and the Comfortable Life in the Bubbles   *141*

8.6. The Diagnosis that Fails to Change the Illusion   *143*

8.7. Technologists May be Useful   *145*

8.8. The Most Dangerous Illusion?   *145*

8.9. How Much do the Politicians Really Understand?   *146*

8.10. Media and Illusions   *148*

Summary Chapter 8   *150*

9. Basic Conclusions   **152**

References   **154**

Foreword

This is a book that is professional but also easily readable for a broad target group. We want this book to be scientifically valid, but because the message is of great consequence for the climate, we also want many people to read and understand the book so that politicians also must take the scientific principles into account. We are compromising between a scientific and a popular style, but never with the truth.

The authors make an attempt to explain the relationships between electrification and the consequences of Norwegian and European measures on global CO_2 emissions. This is important for several reasons, but the most important thing is to explain how and why CO_2 emissions arise as a result of increased power demand in Norway and Europe. Electrification actually has its limitations and we write about that because it is necessary.

At the end of this preface, we have posted a figure illustrating the core of the problem of electrification and CO_2 emissions. Look carefully at this before moving on to the chapters! It explains a key element of understanding "the Last-power", which is an important concept in this book. The Last-power is crucial for everything that has to do with electrification, especially the real, global CO_2 emissions. Today, the Last-power is coal power! "This fact is crucially important for understanding the consequences of electrification."

Another issue of relevance is the Norwegian social model, which is based on trust. This means that politics should build on common sense and proper justifications that stand by professional testing. It may seem like hidden agendas have got too much leeway. Those who have the relevant technological expertise pointing towards misconceptions are not heard. Or perhaps even more importantly: Those who benefit from today's ruling narrative are heard too much?

Social psychology, with an emphasis on illusions, has been given a separate chapter. But what is the connection between illusions and electrification? After working on the topic of electrification and emissions for more than 5 years, the obvious answer is that the reasons and important decisions for electrification are not based on facts, but on established illusions. Illusions, which have attached an iron grip to politicians and government well helped by the electrification industry and the media.

These "correct" illusions have become so prevalent that they hinder the dissemination of objective knowledge about fundamental technology constraints and contexts. Most people are of course influenced by the information they get, which may look reasonable. But the pike lurks as known in the reeds and the biggest pikes are visionary. Critical spotlight on electrification is reflected in the culture that has established itself.

We also have a few words to say about the media's role in the matter. Most of them lack critical interest, have adopted the narrative, and are mostly following the stream, thus preventing any adjustments in the mental deadlock that is riding society in these matters.

The book has two main parts: Part 1: The contexts—includes Chapters 2–6. This section shows how electrification works when used at the wrong time, and how it would work if it was added into the mix at the right time. Part 2: "Bøygen" (the Bend), the late and great Norwegian author Ibsen's symbolic creature which just bends away and thereby hinders *good development* is included in Chapters 7 and 8. These chapters address the problems of breaking through the layers of illusions that protect all the erroneous decisions and consequently, also the unsound plan that will prolong the road to a low-emission society. That narrative-based plan will greatly increase total CO_2 emissions along that road due to inefficiencies and waste of resources.

In Chapter 1, we tell a little about who we, the authors, are since the motives behind us are always crucial to how a message is to be understood. We are well-adult, private technologists, educated at the Norwegian Technical High School (NTH), later becoming the present Norwegian University of Science and Technology (NTNU). Chapter 2 follows the story of why this book came into being from the beginning with a discovery of how we can easily calculate the ratio of emissions from electrified and fossil alternatives, to the realisation that the only way to tell this to a reluctant world was to write a book.

Here, we also bring a link to an approx. 50-page note we wrote in August 2021. This note was written in a series of Norwegian and English editions, and The link is to the last English written version.

In Chapters 2–6, we provide a professional representation of facts that show that electrification today leads to sharply increased global CO_2 emissions.

Chapter 7 shows that climate quotas will not reduce CO_2 emissions when it comes to "difficult times". But they have been useful in making coal power the "Last-power".

Social psychology, with special weight on illusions, is addressed in Chapter 8.

Since this book has a rather complicated structure, we also hope that it will be used as a reference book. The readers will find some repetitions. This is deemed necessary for conveying the comprehensive context of various related aspects.

The target audience for this book is really the whole world; EVERYONE should understand what this book tells. Not everything is easy to understand and you may either believe or doubt our message. Since these are issues of great importance to both Norway and the world, we encourage you to send us your questions via email. Or you can try to figure it out yourself by contacting people with basic skills in physics and chemistry. (Note: It is doubtful whether economists can help in this matter!)

Do you disagree with us? Tell us why: seija-e@online.no

We don't like it but can't resist including a quote from Yuval Harari's book *21 Lessons for the 21st Century*:

Human idiocy is one of history's most important forces, but we tend to disregard.

Last-Power (The Core of the Problem)

The history behind and the definition of the expression "Last-power" is found at the beginning of Chap. 3.3. Likewise, the definition of the word "Infill-power" can be found at the beginning of Chap. 3.4. Please read those chapters now!

The reason for the book being written can be derived from the contexts outlined in **Figure 1**. It shows what happens when power demand increases more than new power can cover. Then the Last-power (coal power) has to be used, and consequently, the CO2 emission increases.

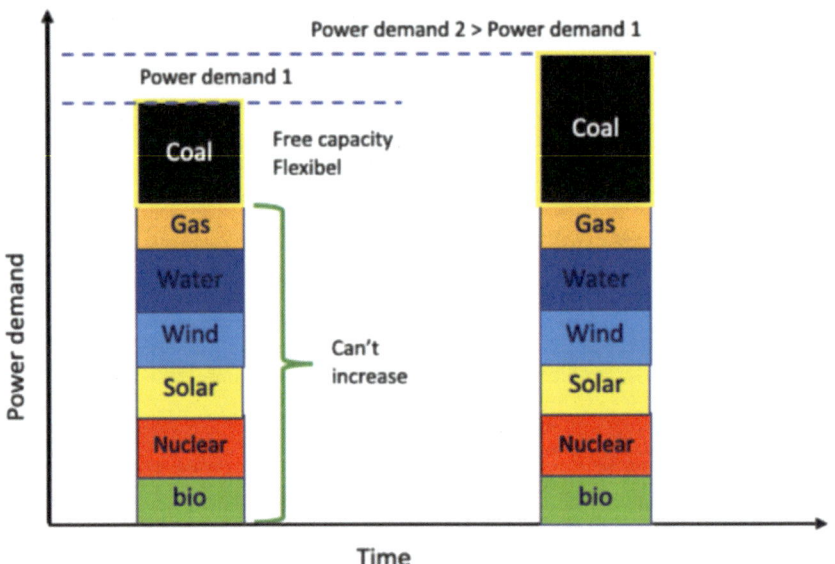

Figure 1: The Last-power determines the consequences of electrification/increased power demand. The figure shows the consequence on the macro level, which is the real climate-relevant level when one ignores all the variable regulatory technical details that in sum do not affect the climate.

Figure 1 explains why all the stories about "zero emission" with which we are bombarded are just illusions. The system response to increased power demand is ultimately taken with the Last-power, which now is coal power. **Figure 1** explains why hundreds of billions of Norwegian kroner spent to stimulate electrification are currently working against their intent. It is too early because coal power first has to be removed.

Figure 1 explains why electrification while coal power is the Last-power leads to increased global CO_2 emissions. This means that it is not possible to reduce CO_2 emissions by "50%" by 2030 because coal power will be the Last-power for much longer than 2030. Without control of the energy balance, and power generation, this will go wrong.

It has proven impossible to get this relationship known through the mainstream media! Freedom of speech, yes perhaps, but the reality is that speech possibilities are limited when not within the "correct perceptions".

Phases into the Future

We have "built" a path to the future, divided into 3 phases with timely measures, which provide the least possible CO_2 emissions along the way.

Phase 1: Coal power is Last-power. 10–20 years duration.

- Stable low-emission power must be increased to the maximum. Development of nuclear power is necessary to achieve the objectives. But we should still wait for the nuclear power of the 4th generation which most likely will be developed over the next 5–10 years.
- Continued development of nuclear power (4th Gen.)
- Coal power must be phased out before electrification continues. Unnecessary electrification increases global CO_2 emissions and exacerbates the power crisis.
- Unnecessary use of electricity, such as electrification of transport and oil platforms must be stopped/minimised.
- Pump power in the EU must be developed vigorously to store surplus power and stabilise unstable wind and solar power. Nuclear power development will reduce this need.

- E-fuels for aircrafts are phased in as low-emission power permits late Phase 3. For large marine vessels, nuclear power will probably become an attractive solution.
- Further development of electrifications. Intensified towards the end of the period.
- CO_2: In Phase 1, electrifications normally will result in twice the emission of the corresponding fossil process, somewhere.

Phase 2: Coal power is phased out and gas power is Last-power. 20–30 years duration

- Custom implementation of electrification can be started during this period, intensive at the end of the period.
- Continued research and development of nuclear power.
- Develop technology for hydrogen power and e-fuels (liquid hydrocarbons made from hydrogen and CO_2) further. Due to the extremely power-intensive production of e-fuels and hydrogen-borne electricity, the transition from phase 2 to phase 3 will have a long duration. If continuing with "today's practice", phase 2 will never end. Implementation is completed in Phase 3.
- Introduction of gas power using oxyfuel technique where CO_2 goes directly to storage. (Without energy-intensive "capture".)
- CO_2: In phase 2, electrifications will, in most cases, emit about the same as the corresponding fossil processes.

Phase 3: Low fossil and low emission, electrification of transport fulfilled. Until the next Ice Age.

- Electrification of air and ship transport by H2 and e-fuels as far as the development of stabilised low-emission and nuclear power permits. It is possible that it would still be appropriate to base most of the air and ship traffic on fossil energy. In this book, we have outlined a possible low-emission use of fossil energy.
- We hope for at least one miracle that simplifies energy production for aerospace and shipping. Large ships can use nuclear power.

- Natural gas will be an important and climate-friendly resource also into Phase 3.
- CO_2 emissions are not gone, but far lower than today for similar energy consumption.
- Unfortunately, those who are not young today are unlikely to experience anything similar to Phase 3. (The illusions mentioned in this book stand in the way of development.)

Summary

Introduction

We show that at the climate-relevant macroscopic level, changes in power consumption today => change in coal power generation. It also means that it doesn't matter who uses which power. Change in power consumption => change in coal power consumption anyway. (Comment: The big mistake in all the major Norwegian reports we have seen about this is that they have not understood/will understand this simple logic and act as if electricity has zero CO2 imprint.)

Chapter 2. A formula for CO2 emissions, and we will write a book.

We prove the formula
[5c] CO2_electrified/CO2_fossil = R(CO2_fossil_electrified) * E_eff_fossil/E_eff_electrified

The formula compares the ratio of emissions, CO2_chain_a/CO2_chain_b from two energy chains. This is found by multiplying the relative CO2 intensity (resource dependent) by the ratio of the energy efficiency of the chains. It is simple, intensities and efficiencies determine the emissions. It actually boils down to multiplying relative CO2 intensity, R(CO2_a_b), with the relative efficiency of two energy chains, accounting for all steps therein.

Inserting real values for the variables in the formula shows that when coal power is the Last-power, globally electric cars emit approximately twice as much CO2 as fossil cars. This applies to most processes. Electrification of oil platforms increases global CO2 emissions possibly even more.

In general: In phase 1, before coal power is phased out, electrifications in general works against its purpose! In phase 2 when gas power is Last-power, a fossil and electrified process will result in approximately the same CO2 emission. This means that it is not urgent to electrify in phase 2, but that we can develop good technical solutions in peace and quiet before electrifying, preferably in the later parts of phase 2 to get the benefits of the improving technology during the period.

Chapter 3. Emissions, electrification and some more.

The problem with unstable wind and solar power is that one must have sufficient Infill-power. This problem is best solved by pump power. About 20% lost energy, but the great advantage of pump power is that it can take care of surplus wind and sun power. Due to the costs, batteries are out of the question for this purpose. This limits how much wind and solar power one can have in a system. *The climate crisis cannot be completely solved only by wind and solar power! On the contrary, in late phase 3, we should have as little wind and sun power as possible.*

Green hydrogen produced by electrolysis as proposed by the EU only shows that the EU does not understand the importance of energy efficiency. Hydrogen production has an energy efficiency of, at best, approx. 30%. When coal power is the Last-power, electric cars running on hydrogen cause approx. 6 times more global CO_2 emissions than fossil cars.

Blue hydrogen producing hydrogen from natural gas still may be a good idea because it offers opportunities for the application of a special variation of Carbon Capture and Storage (CCS) based on the oxyfuel method which can actually work satisfactorily because it also can be a way of storing energy. Today's (when Last-Power is coal power) CCS produces about as much CO_2 as it captures and is completely useless as a climate tool.

The same goes for biofuels. This depends on finding a safe production despite the use of pure oxygen in the oxyfuel process. But it probably gives better energy efficiency to use pure oxygen for direct power generation with natural gas applying the oxyfuel method without going via hydrogen. There are a few gas power plants {1} of this type today.

Then you get a low-emission power source from natural gas. (It will extend the gas age by many years…)

Chapter 4. Time Perspectives

Duration of the individual phases.

	Best case	Probably	Based on existing plans	Optimistic hope
Phase 1	10 years	Forever	30–50 years	10–20 years
Phase 2	20 years	Does not even get into it.	0	20–60 years
Phase 3	Forever	Does not even get into it.	0	Forever

Chapter 5. About realism and feasibility.

CCS should be shut down ASAP. It is far too inefficient and when coal power is the Last-power CCS produces about as much CO2 as is captured.

The oxyfuel method (see Chapter 3.7.5) can be effective if one gains control of the security issues.

Chapter 6. Nuclear power.

The green shift cannot be implemented in reasonable time without extensive use of nuclear power. We recommend, however, to wait for the finalising of development of 4th generation nuclear power plant generators (4GNP). These may apply thorium or waste from classic generators as fuel and will be ready in 5–10 years. They may also be suited for fabric series production of small unities, which therefore will simplify adaption to power nets and may be used in ships. It turns out that this type of power plant can provide relatively cheap energy. It is also shown that the development and production of wind and sun power should be stopped ASAP; they will cause more problems than they solve.

Chapter 7. Climate quotas.

The climate quotas have helped coal power become the Last-power, which has been important. However, these quotas are not guarantors of a low-emission future. They will work only when they are not needed. In crisis cases, like today, they have very little effect. WE MUST HAVE POWER.

Chapter 8. Social psychology.

Explains among other things why illusions are so difficult to get rid of.

Chapter 9 Basic conclusions.

1. A Little About the Authors

1.1 Per

I was born in the Norwegian town of Aalesund in 1941.

After finishing high school, it was natural to start studying at the Norwegian Institute of Technology (NTH) (Today, it is called "Norwegian University of Science and Technology", NTNU). After getting my degree in Technical Physics at the General Department in 1966, I continued as a scientific assistant in the same place. With a family to support and the joyous idea that I was now a civil engineer, the temptation for a somewhat higher salary became too great. I applied for a position as a geophysicist at the Geological Survey of Norway in Trondheim (NGU).

This led to almost 20 years in a nearly perfect job: Constructing new/improving old measuring instruments in winter and spring, applying these instruments in the summer and autumn, interpreting and reporting of results autumn, winter and spring. Fantastic! And here I am tempted to boast a little: Because I used the instruments I designed myself, I knew how they should be and made them like that next winter/spring: The instruments eventually became very good. This was the time close to the start and rapid development of integrated circuits, so you really had to make new instruments more or less every year anyway, just to benefit from the technical development.

In winter, there was even some time to drive a kind of professional development that mainly consisted of developing a model measurement facility, using the same and interpreting the results. There was never time for publication of results as with such a dense program, there was enough unpaid overtime as it was.

In the 70s, it also became evident that Norway would be a large oil and gas producer, so it became natural to take part in the search for these resources. Thus, there was work in GECO in Stavanger. Initially, this work consisted of processing seismic data up to maps which geologists could interpret to find places where there was a good probability of finding oil. It was a fun and exciting job, so time just flew by. GECO was probably glad I was in a job group with no overtime pay.

Professionally, this was a revolution. There are few professional similarities between ore and oil exploration. In ore exploration, I operated with electric potential fields; in oil exploration with sound waves. In the ore exploration, we were happy if we could estimate an ore depth with 20–30% accuracy; in the seismic, we preferably counted on per mile.

Since I had an interest in teaching, during part of my study time, I was active in "Students' Free Education" (SFU) and followed this up with, while working at NGU, completing a course, "Pedagogical Education for Civil Engineers", mainly in my spare time. This provided educational expertise to teach at high school. My wife also worked as a geophysicist in GECO, so when the oil crisis hit around 1986/87, after a rapid risk assessment, the Family Council decided that I should apply for a vacant lecturer position at the electrical department at Stavanger Technical Vocational School.

It was 3½ fun years. I was very impressed with my teacher colleagues. They came almost all from a working life after graduation and were clearly both skilled and motivated. Some of the students were also very clever and some should never have set foot in that school. My confidence in school advisors got a lasting break.

But the oil crisis ended and I couldn't resist the temptation to return to GECO.

My wife got a job in Sandvika in Bærum. The only problem was that GECO was in Stavanger, about 500 km west of Sandvika. Did it lead to a divorce or career stop? Neither, because I soon got a job in Bærum, too: Read Well Services (RWS). As the name suggests, the main mission was oil well surveys, preferably empty of oil and gas. But I never got to work with empty oil wells; I was given the task of handling surface seismic, it was exactly the same kind of work I had done in GECO. But the differences were great. GECO was a big company with a few hundred employees. In RWS, the processing department consisted of 10–15 people.

In RWS, I got a very independent role. Versatile work where pretty much everything that affected the processing I had to do by myself, but with good access to discussions with very capable colleagues. This became my last workplace. I retired but got a long taper of my professional time in the way that

RWS called me when they needed help. No end date was ever set. This was perhaps the best time at RWS, I even got paid for most of the hours I worked.

But I am proud and happy that in both ore prospecting and seismic processing, I could contribute with innovations. In ore exploration with new, simple methods to calculate/estimate the size of electrically conductive bodies, ores, are well hidden in the bedrock. Of course, this was an important parameter for assessing whether it could be an economically viable ore. In the seismic with a significantly improved method of removing multiples (Unwanted sound waves going back and forth between the same reflectors).

But just a short time after I successfully applied my new method in practical processing, an even better method came at hand. It is a shame to lament progress, but it was a bit annoying with so much wasted work, even if most of that work was carried out on my own time.

Apart from a few publications as a result of interdisciplinary collaboration, there was never in question of publishing the result of my ideas: Firstly, it was not possible to find time for that; secondly, they were simple matters. But it was fun.

1.2 Rune

I was born in the small town of Moss in 1959 and grew up in a traditional working-class family. My father worked most of his professional career as a metal and machine worker at Kvaerner Moss Verft until retirement age. My mother was a seamstress at August P. Horn's confinement factory. It was not obvious that I should become an academic.

My interest and curiosity about nature was present as far back as I can remember. Fishing, birds and nature photography are my favourite hobbies. An understanding of the value of nature has grown over the years.

It was not clear until the third grade in high school what the next important step in life should be. It was never an option not to study. Before starting a technological study in Trondheim, one year of military service had to be completed, from 1979–1980. At the faculty of chemistry at NTH, we started with learning a lot of basic chemistry of different variants, as well as physics and mathematics, etc. After choosing the direction of specialisation at the Institute of "Industrial Chemistry", lessons even closer to practical applications in society and industry were followed. Basic principles such as energy balances, mass balances, and thermodynamics were important lessons to take along.

This is highly important knowledge of relevance for the topics treated in this book.

I began at the Foundation for Industrial and Technical Research (SINTEF) right after graduating from NTH, in December 1984; I was then hired by Professor Anders Holmen at NTH. At that time, SINTEF and NTH had large so-called "goodwill projects" funded by the oil companies that wanted to enter the Norwegian continental shelf. At that time, it was a great national focus on looking into the possibilities of utilising natural gas for various purposes. Later on, the focus was on functional materials, mostly catalysts, for controlling the chemistry of various industrial processes and energy conditions. Always on the premises of thermodynamics.

Obtaining a doctorate was a natural expectation. This was completed in 1991 on the theme of production of "methanol from natural gas". The task was to study alternative chemistry that could simplify the way methanol is still being made today. After nearly 40 years of applied energy-related research, my interest lies in issues ranging from the nano- to macro-level of materials. There have been dozens of peer-reviewed publications in academic journals over the years on energy-related issues. The social perspective must always be in the background.

Now we are standing in front of the so-called "green transition". That is a really nice name, but the "green transition" was actually used as a term before anyone knew the practical contents of it.

Unfortunately, the premise of the green shift is largely now being laid by economists who lack the necessary technical and physical understanding. And the motives are not necessarily always "green". Great damage has already happened to valuable nature. Suddenly, there were wind farms along our entire coastline. That is a huge cost for producing well below 10% of Norway's power generation. The wind and solar power are also not trustworthy.

The consequences of basing the future on unreliable power do not seem to be well thought through, as we hope to communicate in this book. In fact, the way electrification is performed under the argumentation of the "green transition" threatens both climate and nature.

1.3 Roy

Roy has been our good friend for many years on and off the badminton court. He shows up along the way with striking comments where needed and puts the closet in place. He has done this for as long as we can remember, with his own ability to see the world as it is. We think we know him well enough that we may guess what he would say in a given situation. He has allowed us to do that.

2. A Formula for CO2 Emissions, And We Will Write a Book

In this chapter, we are providing a method and general tool for the calculation of CO2 emissions from different energy chains. We use electric cars versus fossil cars and the electrification of oil platforms as examples regarding CO2 consequences. It will be shown that electric cars in reality are causing CO2 emissions that are more than double of fossil cars. The same applies to the electrification of oil platforms. Global CO2 emissions double. The readers are invited to look into the detailed calculation via the energy efficiencies of the full energy chains, with a critical view.

The readers that are less interested in the detailed mathematics can easily step forward to following text chapters, taking the main conclusions along.

2.1 We Find a Formula for CO2 Emissions

In this book, we use the abbreviations:

Electric cars:	elcar
Diesel and petroleum cars:	foscar
Energy:	E
Energy efficiency:	E_eff
Input energy:	E_in
Useful output energy:	E_out

Definition of CO2 intensity of a specific fuel, CO2(x)

A basic property is the CO2 intensity of a fuel, i.e., #kg CO2 emitted per produced kWh useful output energy. This is a constant that is dependent upon the specific fuel (gas, oil or coal) and their chemical composition. This is the basic information needed for evaluating and comparing CO_2 emissions of different chains and the consequences of technologies.

$x = 1$ (gas)
$x = 2$ (oil)
$x = 3$ (coal)
$CO_2(x) = $ #kg CO_2/kWh (the intensity of fuel x)
Examples:

1: Methane:	0.207 kg
2: Oil:	0.270 kg
3: Coal:	0.386 kg

Table 2.1:{2} CO_2 emitted pr produced kWh by combustion:

Energy efficiency, E_eff:

We now step further to what happens when the fuel x, with the above-given CO_2 intensity, is converted in a combustion process. The CO_2 intensity is a constant for each fuel, but there are differences in the efficiency of the conversion to useful energy.

Energy efficiency is always a number between 0 and 1 because some loss is inevitably occurring. This compares to numbers between 0–100%. It is calculated [1] as the ratio between input energy and output of useful energy. E_in is the amount of energy of the fuel required to obtain one kWh out.

[1] E_eff = E_out/E_in => E_in = E_out/E_eff

The CO_2 emission per produced kWh of a fuel x in a process (power plant or motor) is then [2] dependent upon the CO_2 intensity and the conversion efficiency.

[2] CO_2-emission = $CO_2(x)$ * E_in = $CO_2(x)$ * E_out/E_eff

Formula [2] is valid only for one single process. For a chained process consisting of more than one step, the E_eff for the chain [3] equals the product of all the individual E_eff. If we have a chain with three steps, we get:

[3] E_eff_chain = E_eff_step1 * E_eff_step2 * E_eff_step3

Since all energy efficiencies are between 0 and 1, the E_eff_chain will decrease for every new step added. Normally, a long chain therefore will have a smaller E_eff than a short chain.

The CO2 emission from the chain, CO2_chain, will be given by [2b]:

[2b] CO2_chain = CO2(x) *E_out/E_eff_chain

The relative difference between the CO2 emission from two energy chains a and b: CO2_chain_a/CO2_chain_b =

CO2(a)/CO2 (b)* E_out_a/E_out_b * E_eff_chain_b/E_eff_chain_a

If we define the relative CO2 intensity: R_CO2(a_b) = CO2(a)/CO2 (b) we get:

[4] CO2_chain_a/CO2_chain_b = R_CO2(a_b) * E_out_a/E_out_b * E_eff_chain_b/E_eff_chain_a

In comparisons usually E_out_a = E_out_b and we get:

[5a] CO2_chain_a/CO2_chain_b = R(CO2_a_b) * E_eff_chain_b/E_eff_chain_a

In plain language, this means that: "The relation between the global CO2 emissions between equally heavy electric and fossil driven cars, equals the relative CO2 intensities between coal and oil multiplied by the inverse relation between their lifetime energy efficiencies".

2.2 Example: CO2 Emission from an Electric Car and a Fossil Car

In this chapter, there are both big variations between, and uncertainty in, most of the variables we handle. Therefore, we normally give results with only two digits. (Even though the calculations are carried out with the available digits.)

Premise: The cars are of the same weight.

From Table 2.1, we find the relative carbon intensity R_CO2_coal/oil = 0.386/0.270 = 1.4

2.2.1. The energy chain for drift of the electric car

E_eff_elcar for drift of the electric car:

[6] E_eff_elcar_chain = E_eff_coal_support * E_eff_coal_power_plant * E_eff_bat * E_eff_elcar

E_eff_coal_support:	Taking into account the efficiency penalty of the chain due to energy used for prospecting, mining and transport of coal to the power plant.
E_eff_coal_power_plant:	E_eff for the coal power plant.
E_eff_bat:	E_eff for the energy loss of charging and renewal of the batteries through the car lifetime.
E_eff_elcar:	E_eff for the electric car, including production of the batteries and heating/cooling of the car.

We have omitted the production of both the electric and the fossil car. The extra energy spent for the production of the batteries, we have put/estimated into E_eff_bat averaged over the lifetime of the batteries.

Estimation of energy efficiencies:

1. **Coal prospecting and mining, {3} E_eff_coal_support.**

For this, we just use the documentation in the linked article and choose that from mine to coal power plant E_eff_coal = 0.85

2. **Coal power plant, E_eff_coal_power_plant.**

Last-power often comes from the oldest power plants with the lowest profitability and efficiency. With time, the influence of this will be reduced. Therefore, we here apply the generally accepted E_eff_coal_power_plant = 0.40.

3. **The batteries, E-eff_bat**

We don't explicitly include the production of the cars in this investigation; we assume that the energy for the production of the cars roughly will be cancelled since it is generally accepted the production of an electric and a fossil car will emit approximately the same amount of CO_2. But that does not include the batteries needed to run the electric car. We, therefore, include a conservative estimation of the energy lost in producing the batteries for the electric car and average this over the lifetime of the batteries. E_eff_prod = 0.90

In addition, we have to add the charge losses and losses in the electric net, which will increase with increasing netload. The grid loss is proportional to the square of the net current. This will, therefore, increase along with the generally increased electrification in the "green wave". A conservative estimate: E_eff_charge = 0.90

The efficiency both of charging and use of the battery also varies with the temperature. We estimate an average E_eff_climate = 0.95

Ageing of the batteries also reduce the effectivity: E_eff_age = 0.95
E_eff_bat = E_eff_prod * E_eff_charge * E_eff_climate * E_eff_age
= 0.90 * 0.90 * 0.95 * 0.95 = 0.73

4. The electric car, E_eff_elcar

An electric car has some of the same energy stealers as a fossil car: The wind (aerodynamics) and the rolling losses, acceleration, and braking. Braking losses may however, to some extent, be reduced relative to a fossil car: Braking by using the electric motor as a dynamo. But depending on the driving style, type of traffic, roads, etc., this of course will take up only a limited part of the lost energy of movement. But at best, this energy on average may be about -5%: E_eff_brakes = 1.05

An electric car must use the batteries also for heating/cooling of the coupe. This, of course, varies very much in Europe, for which this book is written. We estimate that this on average reduces the energy efficiency by about 10%. E_eff_heat = 0.90

Electric motors running at constant load in a free-standing in bench normally have an energy efficiency of 90% or more. We estimate that variable load will constitute at least 5% lost energy. E_eff_motor = 0.85

In sum, we get E_eff_elcar = E_eff_brakes * E_eff_heat * E_eff_motor
= 1.05 * 0.90 * 0.85 = 0.80

5. **Concluding E_eff for an electric car:**

E_eff_elcar_chain = E_eff_coal_support * E_eff_coal_power_plant * E_eff_bat * E_eff_elcar
= 0.85 * 0.40 * 0.73 * 0.80 = 0.20

2.2.2. The energy chain for drift of the fossil car

E_eff_foscar_chain, for drift of the fossil car:

[7] E_eff_foscar_chain = E_eff_oil_support * E_efff_foscar

E_eff_oil_support:	Energy used for prospecting, drilling, transporting and refining the oil to petrol/diesel oil, i.e., a factor describing the energy penalty of the chain.
E_eff_foscar:	Energy needed to run and maintain a fossil car.

Estimation of energy efficiencies:

1. **Oil prospecting, drilling, refining and transmitting. {4}**

As for the coal power chain, we just base the result on the linked report on the subject. Based on this report, we choose E_eff for oil from well to tank: E_eff_oil = 0.79

2. **The fossil car.**

During the last few years, the energy efficiency of fossil cars has improved a lot to now being in the range of about 25% to 35% for petroleum cars and between 35% and 45% for diesel cars. Even if it may look slightly optimistic, we choose E_eff_foscar to be the average of 35%.

Conclusion: E_eff_foscar_chain = E_eff_oil_support * E_eff_foscar = 0.79 * 0.35 = 0.28

2.2.3. Comparison between CO2 emission from equally heavy electric and fossil cars

To compare the global CO2 emission from equally heavy electric and fossil cars, we use equation [5]:

Setting chain_a = elcar, chain_b= foscar and R_ CO2_elcar_foscar, we get when Last-power = coal power:

[5b] CO2_elcar/CO2_foscar = R(CO2_coal_oil) * E_eff_foscar_chain/E_eff_elcar_chain = 1.4 * 0.28/0.20 = 2.0

Here it is time for a conclusion. In plain language, this means that the emissions from electric cars are double the emissions from fossil cars.

2.2.4. What happens when gas power becomes Last-power?

When gas power becomes Last-power, R(CO2_coal_oil), 1.4, will be replaced with R(CO2_gas_oil), the relative CO2 intensity between gas and oil, which is approx. 0.77.

E_eff_foscar_chain remains 0.28 but E_eff_elcar_chain is increased when gas power replaces coal power as Last-power:

From chapter 2.2.2—1. Oil prospecting, drilling, refining and transmitting— we estimate E_eff_gas_support to be about 0.90.

The normal value of E_eff_gas_power_plant = 0.55

E_eff_gas_power = E_eff_gas_support * E_eff_gas_power_plant = 0.90 * 0.55 = 0.50 and => E_eff_elcar_chain = E_eff_gas_power * E-eff_bat * E_eff_elcar = 0.50 * 0.73 * 0.80 = 0.29

When putting the gas-related constants into formula [5b], we get:

[8]   CO2_elcar_gas/CO2_foscar = R(CO2_gas_oil) * E_eff_foscar_chain/E_eff_elcar_chain
= 0.77 * 0.28/0.29 = 0.74

Again, time for a conclusion. Changing the Last-Power from coal- to gas power => electric cars emit about 26% less CO2 than an equally heavy fossil car. But in this calculation, we have *not* included the energy consumption for production of the batteries, in a lifetime perspective, the emissions will therefore be quite equal.

In the general case, one must take into account the emission from any production of new electrified equipment that replaces existing fossil equipment.

2.2.5. The formula is generally valid

[5c] CO2_electrified/CO2_fossil = R(CO2_fossil_electrified) * E_eff_fossil/E_eff_electrified

Example: Electrification of oil platforms.

Equation [5] also applies to other forms of electrifications. A careful examination of both the validity of equation [5] and the values to be used is important for each case. The relative CO2 intensity R(CO2_coal_oil) will usually be for coal-oil, but there may be other opportunities that need to be considered.

An example: Electrification of the *oil* platforms. E_eff_foscar will then be the energy efficiency of the power generators powered by gas (See Chap 2.2.4). The generators applied at the platforms are single-phase gas-driven power/heat generators with energy efficiency of about 0.35.

E_eff_gas_power = E_eff_gas_support * E_eff_gas_power_plant = 0.90 * 0.35 = 0.32

E_eff_elcar will be the energy efficiency of the corresponding electrified process with coal power as the Last-power. But in this case, there is no process, so here we must use:

E_eff_coal_power = E_eff_coal_support * E_eff_coal_power_plant = 0.85 * 0.40 = 0.34

The relative intensity factor R(CO2_coal_oil) (1.4) used for cars must be replaced here by the factor R(CO2_coal_gas) = 1.9 since it is gas that drives the generators you want to replace.

Now equation [5] turns into equation [5d]:

[5d] CO2_electrified/CO2_fossil = R(CO2_coal_gas) * E_eff_gas_power_plant/E_eff_coal_power = 1.9 * 0.32 * 0.34 = 1.8

I.e., also in this case, electrification almost doubles the global CO2 emission.

In a case like this, the problem will be to find the effect of conditions like these:

- The heat from the gas power generators must be replaced by electricity.
- How to calculate E_eff for the production and laying of the cables?

- The extra load of the grid on land for delivering the power by these cables?
- The extra transmission loss in these cables? (Transmission loss increases with the square of the current in the cables.)

All of these factors increase the calculated ratio of 1.8. We can obviously assume that the Norwegian Government is doing a good job at reducing formal national Norwegian CO2 emissions, but a very poor job of reducing real, global CO2 emissions. There are small formalities needed to change an apparent good result to a very bad result.

2.2.6. Manufacture of batteries for electric cars

The range of the electric cars is directly dependent on the size (capacity) of the batteries. But battery production results in large CO2 emissions and is a critical part of the production of electric cars.

Production of the batteries for an electric car emits about half of the CO2 emitted from producing the car. It is questioned whether there is enough raw material to produce the number of batteries needed when all cars and very much else are electrified.

2.3. About the Formula for the CO2 Consequence of Last-power

What about the formula

[5b] CO2_elcar/CO2_foscar = R(CO2_coal_oil) * E_eff_foscar_chain/E_eff_elcar_chain?

Climate models are used to predict what happens, among other things, the temperature in the future.

These are still predictions, a number of unverified versions of a hypothesis. Our formula has nothing to do with either the present or the future. It can be used to compare CO2 emissions from various energy chains, road transport via the oil chain vs. road transport via the electric chain, etc. It can be used to assess the CO2 consequence of Last-power at any time. It is an exact formula based on simple physics and chemistry that shows how things are connected. The formula itself is unquestionably correct, but the results you get obviously depend on having good control over the variables that are included.

The way the variables look today, you will find that electric cars on coal power emit approx. twice as much CO2 as equally heavy fossil cars, and that electric cars on gas power emit a little less than fossil cars. The prerequisites for the formula are based on a fundamental understanding of physics and chemistry.

The relationships between CO2 emissions from the combustion of various raw materials such as coal, oil, and gas are based on fundamental knowledge of chemical composition. The carbon (C) turns into CO2 and H turns into water (H2O) We have assumed that natural gas is pure methane (CH4). In reality, methane typically accounts for 90% of natural gas, along with some ethane and propane. Liquid oil is largely composed of larger molecules built up by chains with -CH2 units. This varies somewhat whether the oil is heavy, light, aromatic, etc., but we think the chemists will say that "CH2" is a perfectly reasonable prerequisite for the composition, so-called stoichiometry.

When it comes to coal, which is a solid, there are also large variations in the composition of lignite, black coal, etc. Carbon content is high but there is also some hydrogen, oxygen, water, and other gruff that affect the energy content and efficiency of combustion. Bad coal approaches peat in composition. 'Not many people understand this' Roy says.

Peat is part of a slow cycle. The other parameters in the formula are calculated from representative efficiencies along the various energy chains, from the oil well to the wheels rolling, from the coal mine to the wheels rolling. All necessary efficiencies in the chains are known, although there are variations for each of these. It is only important to choose reasonable numbers that represent the realities as best as possible. The efficiencies of the power plants for the production of electricity emerge as a result of fundamental energy balances. Production of heat and various forms of losses are taken into account.

This is based on thermodynamics principles and analysis of enthalpies and entropies, as well as some experience data such as charge loss and more. These are well-founded figures. But there is a distribution of the different efficiencies out there in real life, and we try to select values that represent the centre in the distribution. There is no doubt that the ratios we arrive at are close to the right ones. And small variations do not matter to the result and the conclusion, which is robust!

The formula applies on the macro level and provides an overall perspective. CO2 emissions are a global and typical macro-level problem which is what we need in order to understand the consequences of large-scale electrification.

One nice thing about the formula is that it is openly accessible to everyone. The constants used and the functionality is free for everyone to consider at all levels. This means that you don't have to believe, you can easily get into the contexts and make your own reflections.

This is in contrast to the type of models that are so-called "black box", which you have no opportunity to understand, and the most important points are well hidden from readers. In fact, this is not a negligible democratic problem. People are forced to believe as they move into that type of model world. "Knowing or not knowing", a type of problem we have written a bit about in Chap. 8: Social psychology.

To do that, you can insert the values for gas power in equation [8] (Chap. 2.2.4) and get the relationship between emissions from an electric car and a fossil car for that case.

The model does not say anything about quantities and dependencies, such as the consumption of Last-power over a year. To find that, we have to go into time perspective. We have written about this in Chapter 4, it concerns society's ability to establish low-emission power, preferably 4th-generation nuclear power and the ability and willingness to use low-emission power to replace Last-power. We must avoid a situation where using low-emission power is used for electrification only in addition to fossil sources because this will not help lower emissions. The requirement for growth and increased consumption must be reduced. 'Half of what I buy is made in China,' Roy says.

2.4. It Had to be a Book

We must write a book, thought Per. Although our newspaper articles were factual and correct, they did nothing. We never got the last word, and our debate opponents would always focus on irrelevant factors. But one should have a pretty good natural science background and personal integrity to be able to see this. The biggest problem was to get anything at all into the newspaper. One truth doesn't stand a chance against a hundred lies. *Clearly, a book is the only way to be heard*, Per thought. *Full control and all authorisations.*

We, therefore, wrote a 50-page memo about electrification and emissions which we sent to the government, the parliamentary politicians, and most relevant institutes. This led to an online meeting (this happened during the Corona period) with the "Norway's Ministry of Oil and Energy". The only thing we asked for was that the ministry should set up a professionally competent committee to investigate our memorandum. But our actual debate opponents had no real mandate to do anything. This was obviously just an attempt to silence us. Nothing happened.

We have to write a book which kills the illusions, Per thought. *Our message must be so clear that everyone who reads it understands, or at least believes in it. It must clear up all illusions, in Europe to begin with, the rest of the world will come later.*

This was not intended to be a commercial book. It was really meant for free distribution to both EU and Norwegian politicians, where the need is greatest. Absolutely free was fine for us! It's the pleasure of helping that counts.

How many people will understand the book is another matter. Not because it is difficult to understand, but because it tells of a completely different professional reality about emissions than what one people are used to hearing.

As a small afterword to this sad story, we feel that a statement by the Israeli historian and philosopher Yuval Harari fits well:

As bureaucrats accumulate power, they become immune to their own faults. Instead of changing their stories so that they agree with reality, they can change reality so that it matches their stories.

Summary Chapter 2

- A simple formula based on physics and chemistry, which calculates relative carbon footprints for fossil and electrified energy chains, has been developed.
- The formula shows that when the Last-power currently is coal power, today an electric car globally emits about twice as much CO_2 as an equally heavy fossil car. When Last-power is gas power, the formula shows that an electric car emits about 30% less CO_2 than a fossil car.
- The efficiencies in the energy chain and the type of Last-power determine the CO_2 footprint of all electrifications.
- Power without a carbon footprint cannot be purchased from the ACER system. This appears to be a purely economic "fooling system where alibis are sold" only to make money and offer "salvation and cleansing" to buyers.

3. Emissions, Electrification And Some More

3.1. Data for Power Generation and CO2 Emissions

Correct background data from trustworthy sources is of course important. To ensure high credibility and the best consistency achievable, we used only the "International Energy Agency" (IEA) as a source for our figures. The data we found for gas and coal power generation in 2019 is provided below. We find it conceivable that data from 2019 may be slightly more representative of a normal situation than figures from the Covid-19 year 2020. The IEA data is used in the assessments in Chap. 4: Time Perspectives.

In addition, it was estimated by the IEA that in the years 2015–2019, an average of approx. 45 TWh of new renewable power a year was established in the EU. How fast you can manage to establish new renewable power/nuclear power is important for how quickly a restructuring can take place. We believe a historically correct number is far more representative than hopes and beliefs about future production. Since solar and wind power must be followed up by the development of Infill-power, the development of solar and wind power becomes more demanding the greater the proportion of the total power they constitute.

It is, therefore, crucial that solar and wind power do not become a too large share of the total power. We find it disturbing that understanding of this seems to be absent in many circles. Since hydropower is already near its maximum capacity, the only way to do this without extreme intervention in nature would be to build nuclear power. (More about this in Chapter 6.) Since the EU will have problems with sufficient pump power for Infill-power, even with large/vast interventions in nature, it will be difficult to reach the climate target without massive nuclear power development. In fact, it seems impossible.

Gas and coal power production in the EU in 2019 (IEA):

Gas power: approx. 663 TWh

Coal power: approx. 710 TWh

From the IEA figures, we estimate that oil energy used for transport is approx. 2500 TWh. If all transport is converted to electrified transport, it will require approx. 1250 TWh of power because an electric motor is more efficient than a fossil motor. But because of the CO_2 imprint of the Last-power (currently coal power), electrified transport results in far greater global CO_2 emissions than fossil-powered transport. All data must be considered to indicate representative levels that may vary from year to year.

But suddenly, one day, the IEA websites were changed to be useless for our purposes and we had to find other available sources. An alternative source we found was a McKinsey report. {5} It provided the following data for EU27+2 for 2020. (The two countries +2 are Norway and Switzerland.)

Total production:	3500 TWh in ACER
Gas power:	540 TWh
Lignite:	310 TWh
Black coal:	440 TWh
Nuclear:	950 TWh
Renewable:	785 TWh
Water:	475 TWh

The McKinsey report thus says that 750 TWh comes from coal (lignite + black coal) and 540 TWh from gas. For coal, slightly higher and for gas, slightly lower than the IEA figures for 2019. This is data from the Corona year 2020. Either way, the sources seen in context provide a relevant and consistent impression of the situation. Production is distributed at approx. 37% for fossil power, 38% for renewable, and approx. 25% for nuclear power.

We don't want to get into a situation where the power demand is increasing more than the access to new renewable power/nuclear power. We see the consequences today, winter 2021/2022. Energy system, electricity prices and emissions are gone out of control. Society is shaken. Strategic power-demanding industries, such as metal producers, are suffering.

Emissions in Europe are about 10% of the global.

CO2 emissions in 2019:	World:	36,4 Gt
	Europe:	3,4 Gt

The largest emission sectors in the EU are power generation (0,97 Gt), transport (0,83 Gt), industry (0,78 Gt), and agriculture (0,46 Gt).

3.2. Energy Density

The energy content is usually stated as a gravimetric or volumetric density. The gravimetric is the amount of energy in a given amount of substance, e.g., in a kilo. The alternative says how much energy is in a defined volume, e.g., in a litre. Table 3.1 below shows what this looks like for different energy sources and so-called energy carriers. A higher volumetric density value means more compact energy. The values in the table show that the fossil alternatives have significantly higher energy density than those considered future or renewable "solutions". Simply put, it means that the "gas/fuel tank" you need is smaller for the fossil energy types than for the future alternatives.

These properties mean that compact solutions can be established. This is important since free space often is a limiting factor! For some energy carriers, it may mean that there is not sufficient space for the tank or that it becomes too heavy for the purpose.

For example, the data in Table 3.1 shows that it is not advisable to transport wood in the form of wood pellets. It is very ineffective because of the extremely low volumetric energy density. One can transport whole wood 9 times more efficiently. Compared to diesel, you need 10 trucks with wood to transport the same amount of energy as 1 truck with diesel. This says a lot about the efficiency and practical importance of energy density.

The same applies to transport (distribution) of hydrogen since its various forms have very low volumetric energy density. Transport of hydrogen can cause great losses to the energy chain. Any green (from electrolysis of H_2O) or blue (from natural gas w/CO_2 storage) hydrogen will then turn quite black. Therefore, in the chemical industry, it is common to use the hydrogen directly where it is produced. Hydrogen is transported only for special cases and to the smallest possible extent.

(Except goose eyes Norway transporting hydrogen to Norwegian [and northern Norwegian!] from Germany with diesel trucks for use in ferries.

Wonder who made the CO2 accounts for that project? The most likely answer is no one!) The gravimetric energy density of hydrogen is the highest of all. However, volume issues set real limitations for practical use.

It should also be mentioned that the volumetric energy density of Li batteries (NMC, Lithium-Manganese-Cobalt) is very low, in the range of 0.25 kWh/litre. This type of battery is commonly used in today's electric cars. This is a factor of 40 different from e.g. diesel, a formidable difference.

Energy carrier / type	Volumetric [kWh/liter]	Gravimetric [kWh/kg]
Diesel	10,9	11,7
Gasoline	9,7	12,2
Solid coal (black)	9,4	6,6
Liquified natural gas (LNG)	7,2	12,1
Propane (as liquid)	7,1	13,9
Black coal (bulk)	6,3	6,6
Ethanol	6,1	7,9
Methanol	4,6	7,9
Ammonia (liquid, -30°C)	3,6	
Ammonia (liquid, 25°C)	3	
Hydrogen (liquid, -253 °C)	2,6	39
Hydrogen (350 bars)	1	39
Hydrogen (700 bars)	1,9	39
Wood	0,9	4
Battery (NMC - "lithium-ion", el-cars)	0,25	
Wood pellets	0,1	4,7

Table 3.1: Energy densities of different energy carriers

3.3. Last-power

In 2020, we prepared a note: "Electrification: Carbon Footprint and Emissions" {6}. Along with attachments, the note is 51 pages long. It is about electrification before coal power is phased out. There we used the term "marginal-power" which normally is the most expensive form of power. It has later been found that "marginal-power", as we defined {7} it, is used with a slightly different definition in other environments. These environments break the system down in time (hours) so that the marginal-power normally shifts between different types of power over a day. In this book, we look at macro-level conditions, so that marginal-power (now Last-power!) is the power over a longer period of time, from weeks to years.

In this book, we have therefore chosen to replace "marginal-power" with "Last-power" which we define in the same way that we defined "marginal-power" in the note and in the introduction to this book:

In the introduction of this book, there is a brief and simple definition of Last-power:

Last-power is the power we have to use because it is the only available power because all other powers are used to their maximum more or less all the time.

This is illustrated in **Figure 3.1**

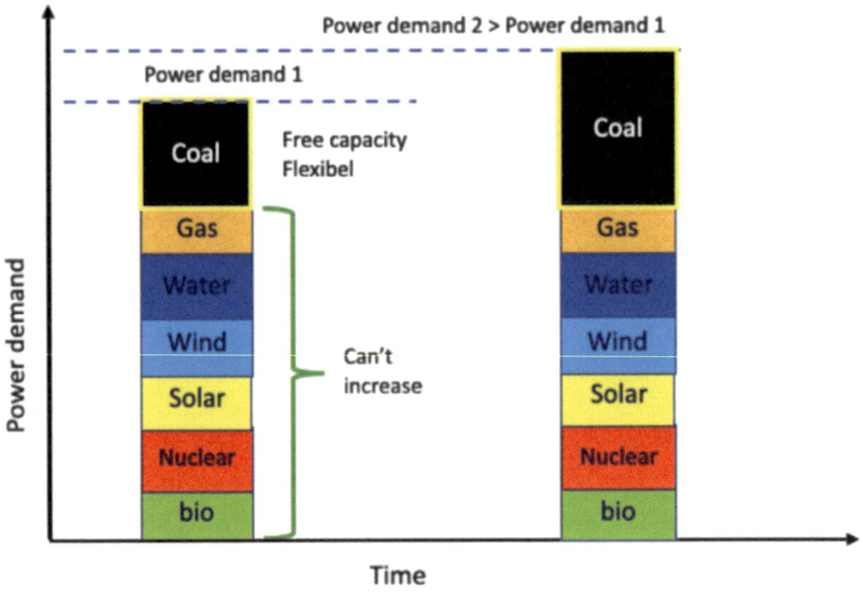

Figure 3.1: The Last-power determines the consequences of electrification/increased power demand. (This is the same figure as in the introduction, but it is repeated since it is critical for the understanding.)

The Last-Power, therefore, varies in line with power consumption. Since money is thicker than CO2, normally the Last-power is the most expensive power.

This is an analogy to marginal tax: "The tax you pay from your last earned money", i.e., "The CO2 emissions from the power we currently use is equal to the CO2 emissions from the Last-power".

A mathematically inspired formulation: The derivative of CO2 emissions with respect to power consumption is equal to the CO2 emissions from the Last-power.

If coal power is not the Last-power, the use of coal power, if possible, will increase dramatically. Since coal power is the power that by far has the largest CO2 emission, about 1 kg/kWh, it is important to ensure that coal power is the most expensive force and thus confirms its Last-power status.

In the note {8} in Chap. 3.3, we divided future time into 3 phases depending on what the Last-power is. We're doing the same thing here:

Last-power:	Approx. CO2 emission:
Phase 1: Coal power	CO2 emissions approx. 1000 g CO2/kWh
Phase 2: Gas power	CO2 emissions approx. 500 g CO2/kWh
Phase 3: Low-emission power	CO2 emissions less than 100 g CO2/kWh

There are, of course, some objections to this. We must clarify the premises:

3.3.1. All other power sources are used to the maximum

It is, of course, not possible to adapt and organise the society to become emission-free. Aspects such as technology, economy, culture and politics all come into play. But what we can say is that if you really want to minimise CO2 emissions, you must strive to get as close to taking account of the Last-power as practically possible. It is obvious that there is much that stands in the way. Coal power has been the most expensive type since late 2019 when coal prices increased due to the increase in the CO2 taxes. This has been so except for a period after the bursting of the North Stream pipes in September 2022.

It is equally clear that the planned large increase in electricity consumption will put greater and greater pressure on the maximum use of "non-coal power energy".

Low-emission energy will continue to be scarce energy. That is why we are talking about the green shift at all. We are firmly planted in a fossil energy system and there is not enough water, wind, solar, and nuclear power to cover the total need. It is in the variable nature of renewable energy that the Infill-power must cover up when the variables decrease. What happens is two things:

- When we increase power demand, renewable power becomes even scarcer.
- In addition, the need for Infill-power increases.

The most important thing is therefore to reduce power consumption and to increase the production of low-emission power in line with the development of the necessary pumping power. The exact opposite is happening. All indicators point to the need for electricity in the future being much larger than today. It will thus become more and more difficult to phase out the types of power that we do not want. Addiction is increasing!

3.3.2. But Norway does not have coal power!

No, we don't have coal power, but we are part of ACER, the EU's common energy market, and the climate doesn't care about national borders. Therefore, the climate will be very happy if Norway sends all the emission-free electricity we have left over to the EU, instead of wasting it on unnecessary electrifications, such as driving a Tesla that increases the CO_2 emission. When the Last-power is coal power, a Tesla weighing a couple of tons will release approx. 3 times as much global CO_2 as a fossil car that weighs half as much.

We simply use up the power or surplus power ourselves "here at home" instead of helping to phase out coal power in the system. This is a simple physical connection in the form of an energy balance which has a clear consequence for CO_2 emissions. Since we follow ACER's rules in the three packages we have consented to, we must follow the same rules of the game as the rest of the EU. Those rules are not illusionary but constitute a clear and distinct reality.

Another very sad matter is that it is precisely the EU that has created the rule that states that emissions must be assessed nationally. This means that, e.g., Norway wants to electrify as much as possible because it is the only effective way for Norway to reduce its national CO_2 emissions. This means that the CO_2 emissions that Norway does not emit will be emitted approx. doubled in the EU's coal power plants.

3.4. Infill-power

Absolutely crucial: *Development of sufficient, reliable Infill-power MUST take place in line with the development of solar and wind power.*

We also used the term "balance power" {9} for this in our note. Like Last-power, the term "balance power" is also used with slightly different definitions in other relevant environments. In this book, therefore, we use the term "Infill-power" instead of "balance power", defined as:

*Infill-power is the power that **must** be supplied when wind and solar power, due to conditions, cannot meet the power demand.*

In any case, CO_2 emissions can be greatly reduced by improving the storage and utilisation of surplus power, which is the power you get when wind and solar energy produce more than needed.

3.4.1. Pump power

In most cases, the best and simplest solution for Infill-power will be to use the surplus power from wind and solar power to pump water back into the water reservoir above a hydroelectric power plant. It may be existing power plants or plants built specifically for the purpose.

The need for new technical installations is minimal. For existing pump power plants, it is believed that there is a pipe system that can be used for water return. Where a return pipe is missing, a supplement must be installed. It is estimated that pump power plants result in a loss of just under 20%. Where existing power plants are used, there may be large distances and therefore some increased electrical transport loss.

Especially Germany has expressed a wish to use Norway's hydropower as Infill-power. This may work even if Norway does not have a large surplus of power because the energy should be supplied from the places that need the Infill-power. Line capacity, on the other hand, maybe a problem. With the electricity prices we have seen lately, this can become a pure win-win situation, without ethical complications for Norway, except that the high prices will charge Norwegian households and Norwegian industry. It will be crucial to find socially acceptable solutions to this.

Pump power probably is the best method for Infill-power today. But in many cases, the capacity is not nearly large enough, it must be developed with such capacity that the demand is covered also for the worst cases of wind and sun-power stops. The reason why the pumping power is so good is that it can store surplus energy from wind and solar power with an energy efficiency of approx. 80%.

However, they can be very expensive to establish if an existing hydropower plant cannot be used.

3.4.2. Battery power

Production and use of batteries for large-scale storage is completely meaningless as Infill-power due to the severe CO_2 emissions and the resource/environmental problems that come with production.

The cost is also crucial: The average price per kWh will be between 10,000 and 50,000 times higher for battery power than for pump power. See details in Table 3.2. BM There are, of course, large uncertainties for the cost of both pump power and batteries. But the difference is so huge that the conclusion is given regardless of uncertainties.

Self-discharge and the limited lifespan of batteries are also a problem. The good and final solutions must be robust and have low operating expenses and losses. Pump power has significantly longer durability and ease of maintenance. It may also be a matter of sufficient raw material access to the huge battery production that will be needed as the electrification of transport increases. (Hopefully, after coal power is phased out.) Of course, good old-fashioned lead batteries are an alternative, but their price is of the same order of size as the lithium-ion batteries.

The Francis turbine is the most widely used turbine type for pump power generators. These can be constructed so that they can be reversed: They can both pump the water upwards and produce electricity as the water goes down. Normally, a Francis turbine will not be reversible. Reversible turbines have fewer blades than the regular turbines. The number of blades depends on the size of the turbine but if a regular turbine has, e.g., 12 blades, a pump turbine is happy to have 3-4 blades.

Table 3.2. Costs for batteries and pump power as Infill-power. The numbers are somewhat uncertain. (Prices in Norwegian valuta.)

3.4.3. Concluding comment

Infill Power	Ah	V	GW	kWh	Total price [$]	$/kWh	Duration [Years]	Yearly price [$/kWh]
Lead battery	100	12		1,2	200	166	5	33
Lithium, max price				15,3	11000	719	15	48
Lithium, min. price		48		7	2200	314	15	21
				TWh	Million $			
Pump, min. price			1,46	12,8	470	0,037	50	0,001
Pump, max. price			0,02	0,16	32	0,21	50	0,004

In 2022, the use of surplus power from solar and wind energy was still an issue of discussion. This shows how primitive solar and wind power is still used even today. But we are convinced that as the relative amount of solar and wind power increases, a more rational use of surplus power, as described above, will force itself forward. In this way, the hydropower plants can increase their annual production, especially in winter and one will always have safe filling of the hydropower plants. With the use of pump power plants, "surplus power" will no longer be surplus power, and all wind and solar power produced will be rationally used, albeit with an approximately 20% loss.

3.4.4. Thermodynamics principles

It has been a long time since man learned to exploit fire. From then on, it became possible to create essential needs such as light and heat. The first people utilised biomass on a small scale and were "renewable" and sustainable by nature. They probably quickly learned what was beneficial food for the fire (fresh, dry, wet, type of wood, etc.). These were the first important experiences of the laws of nature in thermodynamics, which are the basis of human existence today, chemical reaction, combustion to the final products carbon dioxide (CO_2) and water (H_2O), i.e., establishing directly usable energy!

Historically, until "today", the global energy system is almost fully based on combustion to produce power and heat. Combustion of coal, oil, gas, and "bio" for energy production is based on the premises of thermodynamics. Water and carbon dioxide are the zero points of energy. From there, there is no more energy to be gained! Today, man wants to phase in H2O and CO2 to produce H2 and energy carriers for various energy purposes. The energy must come from another source, e.g., from sun or wind. Clouds and meteorological "high pressures" then stand between us and heat/power purposes.

In the energy system in Phase 3, we may want to produce energy carriers from both H2O and CO2 at a large scale. Because both H2O and CO2, according to thermodynamics, are at the bottom of the energy ladder, huge amounts of energy are needed from "external" sources. This means that both energy requirements and losses will be enormous. Normally a very bad deal, since the "external" energy can normally be used far more efficiently directly! It is also uncertain whether CO2 will be widely available at that time.

The use of hydrogen as an energy carrier is strongly promoted today. When hydrogen is incinerated, water is the only product formed. In a narrower view, this has been considered to provide zero emissions. It is common knowledge that hydrogen ignites very easily. This mixture of air and hydrogen is often called "blast gas", and the reaction is very simple, H2 + ½ O2 = H2O. It is a reaction that releases a lot of energy, quickly. No thermodynamic limitations. The "by nature" driving force is strongly in the direction from hydrogen to water.

But the thing is that today, you want to produce H2 from energy-dead stable H2O, i.e., go completely opposite the thermodynamically favoured path. When hydrogen combustion is forced in the opposite direction, the reaction looks like this, 2H2O = O2 + 2H2. Challenging the thermodynamics then has a high price because water is a very stable component.

We can try to visualise what thermodynamics entails. A chemical reaction can be considered a waterfall (like a regular waterfall in nature). An example that follows the laws of thermodynamics is the combustion of methane (natural gas) with excess air, to water and carbon dioxide. It can pass completely (all methane burnt) due to the driving force of thermodynamics. We can join in on the "trip":

You start then "high up at the origin of the waterfall" with only methane and air. Along the way in the reaction of combustion of natural gas, you fall down the waterfall from which you can harvest energy. The higher the fall, the more energy can be extracted. When all the natural gas is burnt, there is only CO2 and water left, and you have then come down to "totally quiet cold water" at the bottom of the waterfall. All the energy is then released.

When CO2 is to be captured chemically, or energy carriers from H2O or CO2 (hydrogen and e-fuel) are to be produced, an extremely large amount of energy must be used. What really is wanted is to turn the waterfall in the opposite direction, upwards. That says a little about how bad the starting point is. And we are "forced" to believe that this *must* be done to the greatest extent to save the world. Hallelujah! But thermodynamics doesn't care about such things. The alternative is to say that the premise of these technologies is certainly not sound. You can say that we have become our own greatest enemy.

3.5. How to Minimise CO2 Emissions

3.5.1. Simple justification for electrification today being powered by coal power

We are currently living under strong electrification pressure. Regardless of what we write, we must expect that widespread electrification will continue. The queue of power-intensive "measures" is growing strongly. But let's still try to arrive at what would be the path to "the emission-free society" with minimal CO2 emissions along the way.

In order to minimise CO2 emissions, we must start by looking at what happens when we increase electrification and power demand. Then we envision a situation that is optimal for minimising CO2 emissions: We use as little as possible of the power that causes the greatest CO2 emissions per kWh: Coal power. This means that when setting the price, we must ensure that coal power becomes the most expensive power and is, therefore, certainly the Last-power. The climate quotas {10} do a good job here. Right now (2022), gas power is probably temporarily the most expensive, but it is also scarce, so coal is still the Last-power.

It also means that if we increase the consumption of electricity, it is coal power production that increases. This is illustrated in a relatively simple way in Figure 3.1. We must, therefore, expect that any increased use of electricity will increase coal power production. (And it is, of course, nice that with reduced electricity consumption, coal power production will decrease, but unfortunately, this is not very likely as it looks now.)

This means that we reduce CO2 emissions to the largest extent by using all the power we can allocate to replace coal power, not for, e.g., driving an electric car instead of a fossil car: Electrifications must generally wait until we have removed all coal power, until we no longer need it.

If coal power is not the most expensive and available power, the use of coal power will normally increase sharply, but currently that is not possible due to scarceness of all other powers. (Reminds that money is thicker than CO2.) It is, therefore, very important to ensure that coal power is always the most expensive available power.

If we are clever, perhaps coal power in the EU can be phased out within 10–15 years. But that requires sufficiently stable renewable energy. That is not the case today. When coal power is phased out, gas power will be the Last-power. Then fossil-fuelled and electrified processes will produce roughly the same CO2 emissions. This will last 20–30 years (or shorter if we are very clever to build 4GNP plants), which means that we have plenty of time to optimise the electrification of the individual processes.

There is, therefore, no reason to push for electrification today in order to be ready until coal power is phased out. On the contrary, it is very smart to wait until coal power is phased out before the development of electrifications begins, then we will have plenty of time and can develop the individual processes with the technology of that time. It will be a big advantage over developing with today's technology. Because in that case, today's technologies will be largely out of date when it would be climate-smart to use them.

3.5.2. About number of steps and efficiency

Each and every step in a process entails energy losses, both chemical and physical. Nothing is 100% effective. From an industrial perspective, the fewest number of steps is therefore sought. Scale, "economy of scale", is also crucial for energy use and thus for the bottom line. Small scale is inefficient.

Almost all hydrogen produced globally today is used directly for the production of chemicals, such as ammonia and methanol, or internally in oil refineries to improve fuel quality. "Direct" means that it is not intermediately stored, it goes straight (directly without stopping and in the right amount—"just in time") to the next catalytic processing step to a product that is easier to store, such as methanol or ammonia. The reason is that intermediate storage requires energy, is inefficient, and therefore disproportionately expensive.

3.5.3. The time of the fairy tales

As children, we grew up with adventures. *Little Red Riding Hood, Hansel and Gretel, The Little Match Girl,* and other dramatic and exciting stories. But we were clever children and somehow understood that the stories weren't real. Imagination is a wonderful quality and it can be used for many things. Today's adventures are of a completely different nature. Now techno-adventures have taken over and adults are the target group. A relatively new trend in society and in the media is all the stories about future industrial adventures. Large, beautiful reports with hundreds of pages are regularly published. These come from various industries, organisations, institutes, and universities.

No need to mention names because they are visible almost every day. Often they are wrapped in a professional facade and contain pompous descriptions of excellence and the potential for tens of thousands of new jobs. This applies to the "Battery Adventure", "CCS Adventure", "Hydrogen Adventure", "Ammonia Adventure", "Ocean Wind Adventure", "Data Centre Adventure", "Crypto-Mining Adventure", and more. A "collected works" should probably be published soon with the title "Electrification adventures collected".

In the mental state, society is in, it's nice to hear fairy tales. But the fundamental reason is perhaps that we have not taken into account the consequences of the fact that electrification increases the use of Last-power. Another good reason not to believe all electrification adventures today is "vulnerability". When "everything is electrified", perhaps sometime in the future, then the system must be protected against all eventualities. We won't have any options to fall back on if electricity fails. More legs to stand on is good in most contexts.

How marketable can technology that conjures up power for far less power be? In the rational world, one can use the term "zero".

3.6. Hydrogen, H2

In this chapter, we will step through the production and use of hydrogen in different ways. The final result is provided in **Figure 3.5** (in Chapter 3.7.4) comparing the efficiency of electrified solutions and consequences for the CO_2 footprint in the present situation when coal power is Last-power.

3.6.1. H2: Chemistry, colours and energy conditions

First, a little general info about the chemistry itself. When talking about hydrogen, it involves molecular hydrogen, H2. It is a chemical compound with a high energy content on a weight basis, a so-called energy carrier. H2 is certainly not an energy source! In the physical space, hydrogen is a colourless and odourless gas. Unfortunately, there are no natural sources of molecular hydrogen that can be harvested. However, there is a lot of chemically bound atomic hydrogen, which must be torn from either natural gas (CH4) or water (H2O) to make the energy-rich molecular H2 hydrogen.

Hydrogen produced in different ways has been tagged by colours.

- Black hydrogen comes from fossils without CCS.
- Blue from natural gas with CCS.
- Green when produced from real renewable power.
- Pink hydrogen comes from nuclear power.
- Turquoise from pyrolysis, which is the decomposition of hydrocarbons to solid carbon and hydrogen.

NB: Since the Last-power today is coal power, the only real colour of hydrogen is black and has the same CO2 footprint as coal power. Since CCS is very ineffective also the blue hydrogen is very dark. When gas power becomes Last-power, all colours will be much brighter.

Abundance and its high hydrogen content make CH4 attractive in this respect. Production of hydrogen today is by far dominated by steam reforming of natural gas. The conventional purpose is not to produce "energy" as such, but society "allows" to use energy to some extent to produce other functional products like solvents, fertilizers, base chemicals, etc.

From water, hydrogen, along with oxygen, can be produced with electricity by electrolysis.

According to thermodynamics, water, like the end product in combustion, is at the bottom of the energy ladder. After all, when we produce energy, we end up with water (H2O) and CO2 as end products.

Hydrogen production by electrolysis and application in fuel cells requires large amounts of energy, causing a total of approx. 70% of the energy to be lost. The total loss up to "H2" is approx. 50%, the rest disappears in the approx. 60%

efficient fuel cell. Production of H2 from natural gas, CH4, results in approximately the same loss. However, this applies to the methods used today.

There already is a working gas power plant {11} with CCS based on the oxyfuel method; it is obvious that this very interesting and possibly very energy-saving method works. The oxyfuel method involves replacing air with pure/enriched oxygen in the combustion process. This means that large savings of energy in the step of capturing CO2 can be achieved this way. For further possibilities with the oxyfuel method, we refer to Chap 3.7.5.

Exploiting also the energy in O2 produced during water electrolysis to "green" hydrogen is a challenge on which there is little focus. In the electrolysis itself, 2/3 of the energy supplied goes up to lift H2 from water on the energy ladder and 1/3 to lift up O_2 from water. The challenge lies in finding applications that benefit from concentrated O2. Here, there can be synergy to be gained by combining this with the oxyfuel method.

Surely, one should have had far more respect for electricity as a highly refined energy form. Electricity is probably at the top of the hierarchy since it can be used for most purposes. Previously (when the society still built on rational pillars), it would be said that it is sacrilege to use electricity for the production of hydrogen, specifically for energy purposes and everything else that involves huge losses. It is thought-provoking that you produce electricity (+ great loss) via H2 from electricity. Many people take it for granted that we always have enough power. We live in spoiled countries for better or for worse.

3.6.2. The carbon footprint of the Last-power

Stakeholders tend so easily to "forget" about the actual footprint of electricity. When the power comes from coal, the production of electricity via H2 gives approx. 3.3 kg CO2/kWh, when it comes from natural gas, approx. 1.3 kg CO2/kWh, from low-emission power very much lower. A fossil-fuel car today emits some more than an electric car on gas power if we disregard the production of the batteries. If the CO2 emission from the production of the batteries is included, the difference between the lifespan CO2 emission from a fossil and an electric car driven by gas power is small.

But today, we are in Phase 1 with coal power—not gas power—as the Last-power. A vehicle that consumes 0.2 kWh/km via H2 emits approx. 0.66 kg CO2/km, about 6 times more than a fossil car. There is, therefore, considerable climate risk with large-scale H2. The "green" hydrogen will not be green before in Phase 3. Used for transport, hydrogen will be much blacker than all current fuels. Only when there is a surplus of low-emission power in phase 3 can hydrogen be an acceptable driving force. The abundance of power today is purely illusory. We see examples of that in the newspaper every single day.

In any case, hydrogen should be used as close as possible to where it is produced. Transport is very unfavourable due to hydrogen's low volumetric energy density (See **Table 3.1**). You have to go all the way down to 253 °C minus to liquefy hydrogen at atmospheric pressure. It can be said that this is the price of developing a market. The market deserves to be developed based on rational criteria.

In the perspective drawn up in this book, it is a paradox that it is the climate and "CO2 reductions" that are used as the main argument for doing so. The low efficiency comes at a price.

3.6.3. Niche possibilities for green hydrogen

As a niche product hydrogen can, of course, be good, for example, indoors and other places where it is required for environmental reasons and where neither directly electrified nor a fossil solution is a better alternative. A good climate justification for hydrogen is difficult to find as long as the power system contains a lot of fossil power. As long as fossil power is needed, aviation based on fuel via hydrogen will emit approximately 3 and 6 times more CO2 than fossil fuel when the Last-power is gas or coal power, respectively. This also applies to large ships. Extensive use of hydrogen must wait until we are well into Phase 3 when there will be low CO2 intensity on the Last-power.

Many people probably also think about the risk of accidents when it comes to hydrogen. It is not unimportant. How many serious accidents will society accept before the use of hydrogen is abandoned?

As mentioned in Chapter 3.2, Li batteries are very low in terms of volumetric energy density. This limits their use to applications where volume and weight are less important. Airplanes are a particularly difficult "case" for Li batteries. Weight is absolutely critical for those who want to fly.

Aviation fuels are the ones most difficult to replace. It could be a rational thought to optimise fossil fuel production for more kerosine in the coming decades.

3.6.4. Use of "surplus power" to produce H2

The concept of surplus power is used as an argument for the use of an initially climate-hostile product such as the production of "green" hydrogen. Since the energy chain based on hydrogen has as low an energy efficiency as around 30%, it needs a reason to be defended. And the alibi is surplus power. Due to the low energy efficiency, the hydrogen energy chain is very unfriendly to the climate, especially since it is intended to be used on a large scale. If someone finds that they want to produce hydrogen far out in the wild without an external energy supply, it is surely an accident of limited dimensions, even if a lot of resources are used which will necessarily be inefficient. But the extent will then be relatively small and insignificant in the climate context.

On the other hand, if you start using so-called surplus power as a justification for the production of green hydrogen on a large scale, much energy will be wasted and much extra CO_2 will be emitted. Resource use will be much greater and thus lead to the use of a lot of electrical energy that is not surplus energy.

Using so-called surplus power to produce green hydrogen is an example of how you cannot always transfer mathematical rules to practical life: In mathematics, we know that minus minus multiplied gives plus. That is not always the case in practical life: "Two follies do not make one wisdom". The two follies in this case are 1) that you do not take care of the surplus energy and 2) that you use an energy carrier with very low energy efficiency. The result is that you waste a lot of energy. The wise thing to do would be to take care of the surplus energy by application of pump power.

In future we may find an alternative for storing surplus power as blue hydrogen by the use of the oxyfuel method, but today this is quite risky. Besides hydrogen is not well suited for storage. Research is needed to find a safe way for applying this method. See however chap 3.7.5

And of course, we may say surplus energy should not be produced at all; wind and sun-power should be replaced by 4GNP as soon as possible.

3.6.5. A small Molboar story from our close reality

We allow ourselves a small diversion. Many people think that molboars (a Danish version of a village of simpletons) are stupid and that we Norwegians are wise. It is an illusion, now proven by Norwegian climate policy. We are just as wise as the molboars.

Proof:

There is a well-known story where a molboar chased a stork out of a field. The stork should not step on the grass, you know. The molboars had a meeting. This was not good. They agreed that they should send out one of them who had small feet, and thus presumably also small shoes, to chase the stork out of the field. There was great agreement in the council: Now we have been wise!

But one of them was extra wise: 'But even he with small shoes will step on the grass!' he shouted just before the gavel fell. Great consternation, this was true! Then they thought for a long time once more. And the extra wise finally found the solution. 'We can carry him out into the field, then he won't step on a single straw.' Six big strong molboars were given the task. They found a gate to carry him on, and then, they carried him out into the field and chased the stork away.

A wise Norwegian climate saviour has probably read and learned from this story. After all, we have ferries in Norway that spew CO_2 into our nice clean air. It's not good, you know. And then he thought for a long time and finally found the solution: "We must use ferries that do not emit CO_2!". For this wise idea, he received a lot of praise, both from politicians and the press. And then he thought for a while and found the solution: "Hydrogen in a fuel cell only releases water vapour!". And hydrogen is easy to make You just put electricity into water and then you get hydrogen. Admittedly, it uses a lot of electricity, but only 3 times as much as is needed to run the ferry with electricity.

Everyone agreed that this was a good idea, and the wise Norwegians made ferries that go and go without emitting a gram of CO_2! And if they haven't stopped celebrating this success, they're still celebrating.

But in a completely different country, they made electricity with coal power, and they discovered that the need for coal power was increasing and increasing all the time. "But never mind," they thought, "when the ferries ran on electricity, we earned twice as much money. Because the electricity we create, and which the ferry uses, emits twice as much CO_2 as a diesel ferry and the electricity that makes the hydrogen the ferry needs, emits six times more CO_2 than a diesel ferry. So now we earn six times as much money as when the ferries ran on diesel."

"It is the wise Norwegians who keep us in business," they thought, but they didn't say it out loud, because some really wise people could think a little more.

3.6.6. Scale considerations

3.6.6.1. EUs headless plans

The EU has ambitions, huge ones, for green hydrogen, i.e., produced by electrolysis. Green hydrogen is not considered a niche at all because the ambition is to replace both oil in transport and coal and gas in power generation. They really haven't understood the "CO2 consequence" of their plans. The competition to be "best at setting goals" is fierce. Politician mentality has this unfortunate side. It is obvious that the energy price (incl. CO2 emissions) that must be paid for hydrogen to such an extent is too high. It must certainly not be carried out to such an extent as long as low-emission electricity is in short supply. It really would have been a crisis both for climate and infrastructure dependence.

Steering money flows in the direction of the EU money bin may be another not insignificant success criterion. 'Money is power,' says Roy.

For the best understanding of some of the following sub-chapters, it is important to be aware of state-of-the-art, the present situation for H2 production and use. Hydrogen is produced at a large scale today, according to **Figure 3.2**, mainly from natural gas steam reforming, partial oxidation of other hydrocarbons, and even to a large extent by coal gasification. The global annual production is around 120 Mtons. These fossil-based production routes constitute 96% of the hydrogen cake, while the green (electrolytic) desired method, intended to replace the other methods, is as small as 4%.

The largest uses of hydrogen are for ammonia, methanol, and for internal needs in oil refineries. This is hydrogen that goes directly from the production step to the next chemical step, without storage and transport. That is the efficient way of doing it.

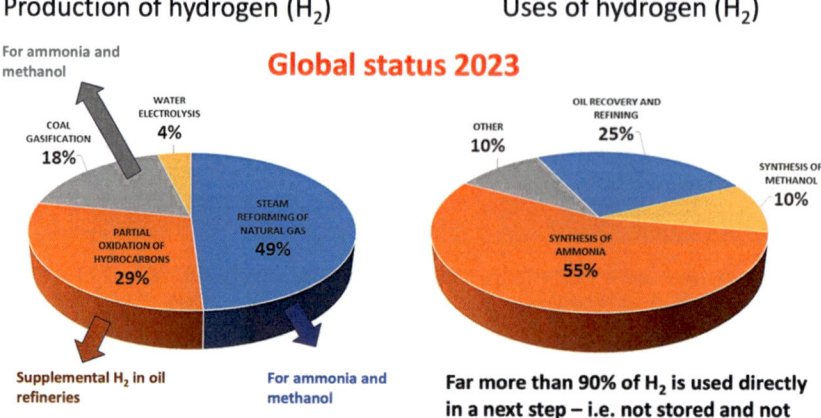

Figure 3.2: State of the art for hydrogen production and application. When later coming to e-H2 (H2 produced via electrolysis), e-NH3 (produced via e-H2 and nitrogen separated from air), and e-fuels, this belongs to the electrolytic way of producing e-H2, equal to the "4%" share in the figure.

3.6.6.2. Consequences of H2 export and efficiency

A theoretical exercise! Looking more closely at scale implications! If we choose to export H2 only instead of methane in today's "pipe-grid" connecting us to Europe, the amount of energy exported will drop dramatically (Natural gas consists typically of about 90% methane). This will be outlined in the following. Today, Norway exports significantly more than 1,000 TWh annually in the form of methane. A separation of carbon and hydrogen in methane will have large consequences.

Separation of methane to hydrogen: CH4 => 2H2 + C.

About 50% of the total harvestable energy in CH4 is in the 4 H-atoms, converted to 2 molecules of H2 in the stoichiometric reaction equation (factor 0.5). In the reaction above, solid carbon is the other product. Less energy is then obtained since the energy release of converting C to CO2 is not harvested.

But since the pressure of a gas volume is independent of the weight of a molecule, only on the number of them, the 2H2 will take double the volume of the original CH4! This means that this physical property alone halves the capacity of the "pipe-grid", i.e. by factor 0.5

Then there is another fact, i.e., that the volumetric density of hydrogen is only 31% of methane (factor 0.31).

The capacity of the grid for energy transport of hydrogen compared to methane, if fully replaced, will therefore be:

0.5 * 0.5 * 0.31 = 0.078 = 7.8%

More than 90% of the capacity of energy transport is lost! Conclusion:

The capacity for energy transport of the "pipe-grid" for hydrogen is only 7.8% of the capacity of the methane.

Besides hydrogen demands better qualities both for the pump and for the compression.

The original energy export of 1000 TWh/year by methane (natural gas) will, via replacement with hydrogen, be reduced to about 80 TWh/year.

This is a really dramatic decrease in yearly energy exports. If the hydrogen in the other end of the export pipe ("in Europe") is to be used in an H2 power plant (efficiency 55–60%), or in an electric car with a fuel cell (efficiency 60%), then the usable power will be reduced to about 50 TWh, about 5% of the original energy. This illustrates that the proposed "H2 export concept" results in access to dramatically less energy in Europe, which is not in accordance with today's needs, since the situation at present is a problematic energy deficit, demanding the most effective solutions. The concept of H2 export is based on pure symbolism (fitting well into the correct narrative) and not a rational energy strategy.

When it comes to the proposal for a hydrogen pipe to Europe, the volumetric energy density of H2 and CH4 is crystal clear: *Hydrogen must be produced at the end of the pipe where the methane comes out.* Everything else is energy madness. In any case, this will have to be put aside due to material aspects and costs. It is pure symbolism and obfuscation that we could do without.

If all the natural gas is converted into hydrogen to be exported with special trucks, it will require approx. 40 million transports per year for compressed gas or 12 million per year for liquid hydrogen. Keeping in mind that both compression and liquefaction will consume a proportion of the energy.

The liquefaction process itself typically requires about 20% of the energy provided by the hydrogen. If it is done on a small scale, it will require an even larger share.

What about transport by shipping, as an alternative, still considering the full export scale? With a capacity of 500 tons of H2, it will require 86,000 shiploads per year. It will be busy in Norwegian ports and cramped at sea. One may of course build larger ships, but in 2019, this size was on the drawing board at a Norwegian shipyard.

The fundamental aspect is that hydrogen, in reality, is not suitable either for storage or transport on a large scale because it is inefficient, technologically advanced, and therefore also very expensive.

The differences between green and blue hydrogen

According to open sources, it takes approx. 50 TWh of power to produce 1 Mton of electrolytically produced green H2 (about. 50–55 kWh/kg H2 is the representative power requirement).

Again considering the total annual Norwegian export scale of natural gas. Theoretically, ca. 40 Mtons of H2 can be produced annually by steam reforming 121 billion m^3 of natural gas.

Thus, the power required is 50 TWh/mill. tons * 40 = 2000 TWh (green H2). Put into perspective, the whole European power system is approx. 3000 TWh. The power to do such a thing at a significant scale does not exist. One can surely say that there are illusory thoughts behind the hydrogen strategies in Norway and Europe (as pointed out earlier and which cannot be repeated often enough).

Moreover, as long as the Last-power is coal power, the use of 2000 TWh of power will mean 2000 Mtons of CO2 produced. But it is still called green!

Aspects related to scale

As an alternative to using power, hydrogen can be produced by conventional means, i.e., via natural gas reforming. Again looking at the scale of exports and evaluating how many plants would be needed for converting the natural gas to hydrogen. Today, the existing plant at Tjeldbergodden in Norway is representative as the industrial scale. This plant is producing methanol (for chemical purposes) but with hydrogen and carbon monoxide as intermediates, produced by steam reforming. The plant "consumes" about 0.7 Gm^3 of natural gas annually. Comparing with the annual export of ca. 121 Gm^3, it means that ca. 200 plants of this size in continuous operation will be needed.

This is further illustrating that it is completely unrealistic due to the enormous scale of the existing "export" system. It is possible on a small scale but with no impact on the existing "energy export" system.

On the other hand, the production of blue hydrogen by steam reforming means that 121 Gm^3 of natural gas is converted into 238 Mtons of CO2. That number is large and approx. 5 times greater compared to the annual Norwegian emissions, which is close to 50 Mtons.

The energy required to capture CO2 with "CCS" varies, but a realistic figure from open sources is that it takes approximately 1 kW/kg CO2. This means that if you use electric power, which will be the Last-power, as much CO2 is emitted as is captured; in other words, a gigantic waste of power for absolutely no use. By use of the oxyfuel method (Chap. 3.7.5), the "CCS" avoids the step of capturing CO2. If low concentrations are to be captured, more than 1 kW/kg CO2 is required. That figure means that it will take more than 238 TWh to capture 238 Mtons of CO2. That figure is far higher than the annual power production in Norway, which is between 140 and 150 TWh. 238 TWh amounts to approx. 20% of the calorific value in the entire Norwegian annual gas export.

3.6.7. Hydrogen as a greenhouse gas

Hydrogen has not been considered a greenhouse gas, but recently, knowledge has emerged {12} that it can indirectly act as a greenhouse gas by preventing the breakdown of methane, CH4, in the atmosphere. (H2 reduces ozone O3 and OH which would normally have helped to remove the methane.)

One must, therefore, be particularly careful to avoid large hydrogen leaks.

3.6.8. A small story about today's sad Norwegian hydrogen illusion

Norway's government is very fond of the idea of hydrogen pipes for Europe. Equinor wants effective ways to export hydrogen (and they don't care how). They want large plants in Norway (10 times of Tjeldbergodden) and pipes out of the country.

However, the problem is that the transport of hydrogen is very inefficient. If you replace natural gas with hydrogen in today's pipes, the amount of transported energy pr. year is reduced to about 8% due to the lowering in energy density and reduced transport capacity in the grid as shown in Chap. 3.6.6.2.

This simply means, in a rational perspective, that the hydrogen must be produced on the "other side of the pipe", at the receiver end where the natural gas arrives, not in Norway. In addition, hydrogen causes material problems for pipes and equipment. Metals become brittle. Pressure is a problem.

Overall, it is expensive and not rational! There is no quality assurance at the political level today that puts these things in place professionally.

3.7. E-fuels (Liquid Hydrocarbon) and Ammonia

The "captured" combustion product CO_2 is promoted as a significant resource in the future energy system. Through chemical capture and reaction with green or blue H_2, e-fuels, chemicals, and materials are to be produced. As for the combustion product H_2O, the thermodynamics of CO_2 is very unfavourable as explained in Chap. 3.4.4.

Furthermore, challenges in the synthesis (controlled building of new chemical bonds to form desired products from the starting materials) of e-fuels with regard to energy needs are due to chemical constraints. The synthesis step from H_2/CO_2 to hydrocarbons (representatively built up by $-CH_2$ units) is very demanding in that products other than those you want are favoured. The first two H_2 molecules react with the two O atoms in CO_2 and reproduce two water molecules, which are more thermodynamically favoured. Hydrogen atoms from the third H_2 molecule can attach to a C atom.

This means that a maximum of 1/3 of the hydrogen in the feed enters and becomes part of a hydrocarbon product. That factor alone makes e-fuels 3 times less efficient than hydrogen directly. It must be used 3 times more power for electrolysis than is necessary for the use of hydrogen alone. Such a loss in efficiency matters!

What is promoted as energy solutions for the future requires a great deal of energy input, it does not release energy at all. It is pure waste, and where is all the energy this requires? Dream on!

Preparation of e-fuels, liquid hydrocarbons, requires, for fundamental reasons, at least 3 times more energy than the production of hydrogen alone. This means that the energy efficiency for this step alone is a maximum of approx. 10%. Since this is a fact given by nature itself that we cannot avoid; no matter how long and skilfully we research this, this relationship cannot, for fundamental reasons, be significantly more positive. In practice, the 10% is reduced to about 5% due to losses in a long chain of operations. We are, therefore, not moving forward with this field here. But once the Last-power becomes low-emission far into Phase 3, and we have a big surplus of it, this can be considered again and see if it can improve the current power options at that time.

Ammonia is considered to be a good energy carrier for hydrogen.{13}But why use an energy carrier for hydrogen, why not use hydrogen directly? The reasons for this are handled in Chapter 3.6. The three main reasons are transportability, storage problems and safety. In this respect, the two first reasons, ammonia is much better. Today, large quantities of ammonia are handled in existing infrastructure. Both liquefaction and shipping are possible. But using ammonia as an energy carrier comes with a prize:

Use of ammonia as an intermediate H_2 carrier for fuel-cell applications is about 3 times less efficient than direct H_2 and 9 times less efficient than direct electrified transport. See **Figure 3.2** in Chapter 3.6.6.1 and **Figure 3.4** in Chapter 3.7.1 for a comparison of hydrogen and ammonia energy chains, including major steps required and final usable energy. But one limitation that is talked about too little is the toxicity of ammonia. We really need a leak-free society. The electric value chain (see **Figure 3.4**) demands huge amounts of power.

When the Last-power is used, which today and for decades to come is coal power, the efficiencies and consequentially real CO_2 emissions must be calculated in light of this.

3.7.1. About power production, emerging alternatives

Gas power involves completely burning methane directly into CO_2 and water (end products in today's energy system). Out you get electricity and heat. Releasing CO_2 directly into the atmosphere requires no energy. (In contrast to CCS.) Gas power plants can be up to 60% thermally efficient, which means that this proportion of the energy input is utilised for power. Further transmission of the power the need to possibly convert direct current into alternating current and transform up to high voltages, are losses that must be taken to reduce transmission losses.

Power plants based on blue hydrogen as fuel require that H_2 is first produced in a process step, e.g., by steam reforming of methane to H_2 and CO_2. The loss in this step is approximately 20%. In addition, liquefaction for storage, drying, pumping or compression. Pure CO_2 can be liquefied by compressing it to 57 bars at room temperature. Transport of hydrogen, especially in gaseous form is, as mentioned above, inefficient due to its low volumetric energy density. The hydrogen must then be burned in a separate step to generate power and heat. A lot of energy is then lost on the road due to many steps that either require more "energy in" or in the form of losses as a consequence of chemical reactions.

'Bad deal to produce little power from a lot of power,' says Roy.

However, when coming to alternatives for producing chemicals and fuels. Today, dominantly used as chemicals, H_2, NH_3 and CH_3OH (methanol) are also suggested to be fuels of the future. Today, diverse fossil sources are dominantly used for the production of ammonia, methanol, and other bulk chemicals. The alternatives strongly promoted today are suggested to produce by starting from power, water and CO_2, and the target is to replace large-scale production routes from fossil ones.

However, as **Figure 3.3** shows, the share of the present route from water is extremely small compared to the conventional, i.e., 4 vs. 96%. However, it is not part of the figure illustration that hydrocarbons today (kerosine, diesel, gasoline fractions, i.e., fuels) are mostly produced by oil separation and refining. Only a minor part is made synthetically.

For the conventional routes, the major amount of energy needed to produce the hydrogen or the mixtures of H_2/CO and H_2/N_2 is supplied by heat from either external or internal combustion reactions. That means that part of the fossil feedstock is used for generating the required energy (heat), thus also being the reason for significant CO_2 emissions. For steam reforming, external burners are typically used to supply heat for achieving reforming temperatures of 900–1000 °C. The conventional routes use some electricity as well for compression, pumping, separations, etc. The electrolysis routes are based exclusively on power as energy type, and then the consequential CO_2 emissions are highly dependent upon the footprint of the power system (Last-power).

Although the energy efficiency for hydrogen as an energy carrier is around 30% for both the conventional route and the "electrolysis" route, today the conventional route emits CO_2 through production, while the "electrolysis" route emits even more CO_2 through heavy use of Last-power. Since electricity is currently in short supply and we have plenty of fossil raw materials, the conventional route should be preferred. However, in Phase 3, the CO_2 footprint of power is reduced and the "electrolysis" route is likely to be preferred.

In liquid e-fuel production, a proportion of the end product in the chemical synthesis. Meaning of synthesis in this case is facilitating the combination of the

H-atoms with the O and C atoms in CO2 is hydrocarbons with a high energy density (gas, petrol, diesel, and heavier ones up to wax). From these, liquid fuels can be produced that are compatible with existing infrastructure and use. That's the benefit but not the whole story. To get to the finish line from water and a CO2 source, a large number of steps are required:

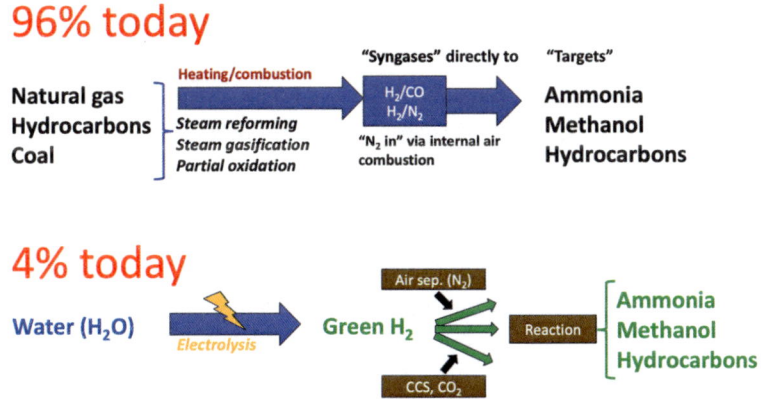

Figure 3.3: Overview of present routes to ammonia, methanol, and hydrocarbons.

- Hydrogen is normally produced from natural gas with subsequent handling (several steps). CO2 must be captured to be made available.
- In the synthesis from H2 and CO2, besides losses due to H2O formation, hydrocarbon gas fractions (methane, ethane, propane, butane) will be formed, perhaps a petrol and diesel fraction (possibly kerosene, jet fuel). These must be distilled to the correct boiling point range. The kerosene has a "narrow", boiling point of approx. 190–250 °C, and hydrocarbons with a number of carbon atoms from 9 to 16. Cold properties are absolutely critical, behaving as an easy-flowing liquid at -50 °C.

What is formed from heavier hydrocarbons, the long chains must be split up in a separate step, which also requires energy. It is a chain of events. This further reduces efficiency. In addition, the various products must be certified to become products that can be used.

- The efficiency (carbon utilisation, i.e., share of carbon) of a specific fraction, such as, e.g., jet fuel is limited by its chemistry.

Ammonia (NH_3) is popular as an energy compound under consideration for several types of applications. Today about 80% of the produced ammonia is used as fertiliser. Ammonia is being considered as a possible future fuel, especially for marine use in internal combustion engines. As described above, ammonia is also a so-called hydrogen carrier, which can optionally be split into H_2 and N_2. H_2 can then, among other things, be used in fuel cells for the production of electricity for various applications.

Typically, all the steps required from hydrogen production to application will lower efficiency. For example, ammonia power plants require even more steps than hydrogen power plants. Blue hydrogen is produced as mentioned above, but in addition, N_2 and O_2 must be separated, either by means of "pressure swing" or possibly cryogenically (N_2 becomes liquid at -196 °C), or by using chemical methods. Next, H_2 and N_2 must be compressed to between 100 and 450 bar (an important step) and reacted (synthesis step, facilitating chemically combining N and H-atoms) to ammonia. Liquid ammonia, which has a limited volumetric energy density, must then possibly be stored (step) and transported (step).

The ammonia must then be split into hydrogen again (step) or burnt (step). The exhaust may need to be cleaned, i.e., removal of NH_3 and NO_x (stage). Even more energy is lost on the road than for hydrogen alone. 'That was many steps,' says Roy, 'and even less power from power. I hope we don't need to understand and remember this.'

Small plants require additional energy use for transport and storage. Then the efficiency becomes poor. As shown earlier, hydrogen should be used close to where it is produced.

When we look at green hydrogen on a large scale, for example, to achieve 7 TWh of usable electricity via H_2, it demands approx. 20 TWh power. "Electricity (+ loss) from electricity" via H_2 is therefore only "sustainable" when the benefit is considered more important than the energy lost. Using electricity directly is much more efficient, at least 3 times. It should then be possible to understand that this is pure waste. It gives associations to the luxury trap where one has lost an understanding of the economy and control over consumption.

A comparison of the processing steps for the suggested future electric-driven energy chains of hydrogen, ammonia, and liquid e-fuels is provided in **Figure 3.4**, in Chapter 3.6.6.1.

Production of e-H2 e-NH3 and e-fuels (liquid hydrocarbons) are linked, as the figure shows. The primary key to ammonia and also liquid e-fuels is the availability of hydrogen. For ammonia also N2 is required, and for e-fuels also CO2 is required.

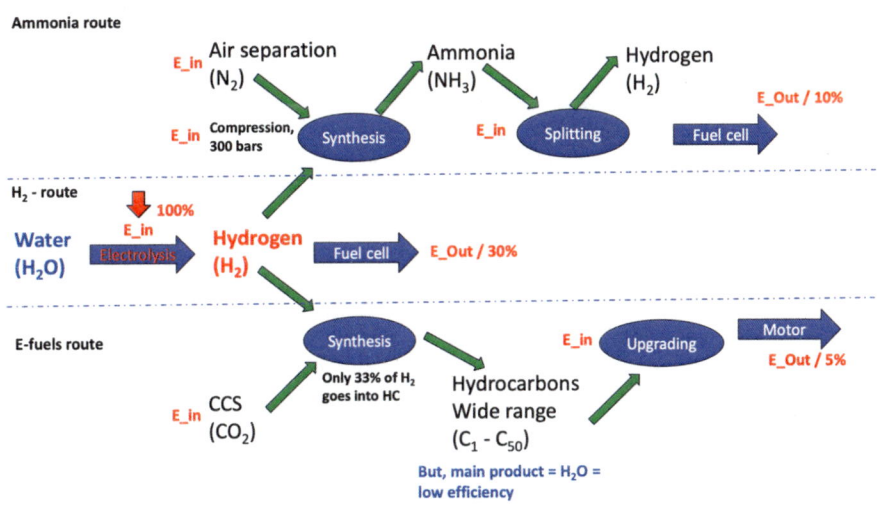

Figure 3.4: "Future is electric", A comparison and relations between three electric chains to e-H2, e-NH3 and to e-fuel liquids.

In Figure 3.4, we show the production of hydrogen by electrolysis of water, and how e-H2 is a key also for the electric chains to e-NH3 and e-fuels energy. This is the alternative suggested by top EU politicians to the present conventional technology for ammonia production, which is based on natural gas conversion for producing H2. See figure 3.2 in 3.6.61.

The reason for the high-power needs in the e-routes is visualised in **Figure 3.4**. Use of H2 "directly" involves fewer steps than for NH3 and the e-liquids, but significant losses of 70% of power occur in production due to handling and the fuel cell, primarily. For the e-NH3 chain, the very high pressures, air separation, compression and e-NH3 production steps give energy losses. For fuel-cell applications, the ammonia must also be broken down again to H2 and N2. Useful power out is only 10% of the input power, rather inefficient. For liquid e-fuels, because of fighting with the bad thermodynamics of CO_2, even less useful energy is established in the end. In the hydrocarbon formation reaction (synthesis), the combination of H_2-atoms with O and C in CO_2, two H_2O molecules are reformed before the hydrocarbon fragment H-C can be established. This ends up with less than 5% useful energy.

Conventionally (fossil route), the right amount of nitrogen is made available by integrating partial combustion with air in the natural gas conversion step. Both nitrogen and hydrogen are subsequently reacted directly to ammonia, i.e., the H_2 (and N_2) is neither stored nor transported. The energy needed for the conventional route is approximately 9500 kWh/tonne (energy mostly from natural gas) compared to 12000 kWh/tonne (energy mostly from power) when using electrolysis for the hydrogen production and power/heat for a dedicated air separation step.

3.7.2. Toxic fuel on the tank

Visions of zero emissions are popular today. A zero vision that must be followed in practice is a leak-free society. It is never mentioned but most people with an interest in technology know that ammonia should be treated with great respect. Leaks cannot be tolerated because ammonia is fatal at low concentrations, around 300 ppm (parts per million). The challenge is that ammonia has a boiling point of -33°C and it is a gas at normal pressure and temperature. Anything that leaks out of a liquid ammonia tank will turn to gas, which has the potential to spread quickly. A small volume of liquid becomes a much larger volume of gas. And materials must be chosen carefully as ammonia is basic and corrosive. "Corrosive—gas—toxic", is a very bad combination.

One reason why ammonia has gained focus is that the molecule itself does not contain carbon atoms. Thus, it is incredibly easy to market.

The big question is where ammonia can be used, in a sufficiently safe way. The maritime sector is mentioned most often. The fairy tale says that it will replace much of today's fossil fuels. The fairy tale also says that it will happen quickly, it's just a matter of getting started. We don't think that will happen. "Unforeseen obstacles" will limit the scope, such as the fact that the total energy efficiency is significantly lower than hydrogen alone. The Health Safety and Environment (HSE) requirements that follow safe handling and use will also contribute to strong limitations.

Funnily enough, for decades society has developed technology to remove low residual concentrations of carbon monoxide (CO) from exhaust gases due to its toxicity. Like ammonia, carbon monoxide has a toxicity that should not be messed around with, a few hundred ppm is the limit. When ammonia is to be used as fuel, the same problem will arise. Unburnt ammonia must be removed or handled in another way. Engines optimised for ammonia are still under development. This is not a mature technology and who knows when, or if, it will be?

One can almost conclude that CO as a fuel is now the ideal. You burn CO to CO_2 with concentrated oxygen and get pure CO_2. The pure CO_2 can of course be electrolysed back to CO and oxygen, and thus you have the ideal energy cycle. Had it not been for the toxicity of CO, using CO as an energy source could have been a good proposal.

A container ship will use 8.500 tons of ammonia just one way between Amsterdam and Shanghai. A little use of a pocket calculator will show that if one were to run the 580 largest container ships on green ammonia, Europe would use half of all its power production to make this green ammonia.

3.7.3. E-Ammonia production from an energy perspective

Today, ammonia is a large volume industrial bulk chemical, of which 80% is used for producing fertilisers, some for refrigerant use, explosives, and a number of other chemicals (not energy). Ammonia and fertilisers are crucial for food production. However, now ammonia is also proposed to be used for energy, for H_2 and also to be used directly as a fuel, potentially an e-fuel in the marine sector.

We can do the same exercise again as above, relating energy requirements to production at full-scale replacement of Norwegian natural gas exports.

Production of green ammonia (e-NH_3) is based on green hydrogen (e-H_2). It will require ca. 1000 TWh to produce 242 Gm^3 e-H_2 as is obtained from the thermal splitting of 121 Gm^3 of methane.

Comment: If considering steam reforming, the amount of hydrogen would double to 484 Gm^3 because it is produced from both methane as well as from water. 2000 TWh would then be needed in the electrolysis. The 242 Gm^3 H_2 annually is 20 Mtons by weight. The molecular weight (Mw) of ammonia (NH_3) is 17, which means that this amount of hydrogen has a potential for the production of 93 Mtons of NH_3 It requires 73 Mtons of N_2, which is another challenging issue. By comparison, the annual global ammonia {14} market is somewhat over 240 Mtons, expected to increase towards 2030.

In addition to the power needed for green H2 production with electrolysis, more power will be required for other things in addition to various losses in the chain. To produce NH3, pure N2, separated from air, is required (see Fig 3.3). This can be done either cryogenically (by low temperatures) or with a technology called pressure swing. Hydrogen and nitrogen must then be compressed to very high pressures (300–400 bar) to carry out the classical catalytic synthesis (Haber-Bosch). According to Wikipedia, the power needed is approx. 0.39 TWh per Mtons of N2 separated from the air.

Also according to Wikipedia, the minimum theoretical amount of energy to compress hydrogen isothermally to 350 bar is 1.05 kWh/kg H2. Theory is one thing but consumption will be greater in practice.

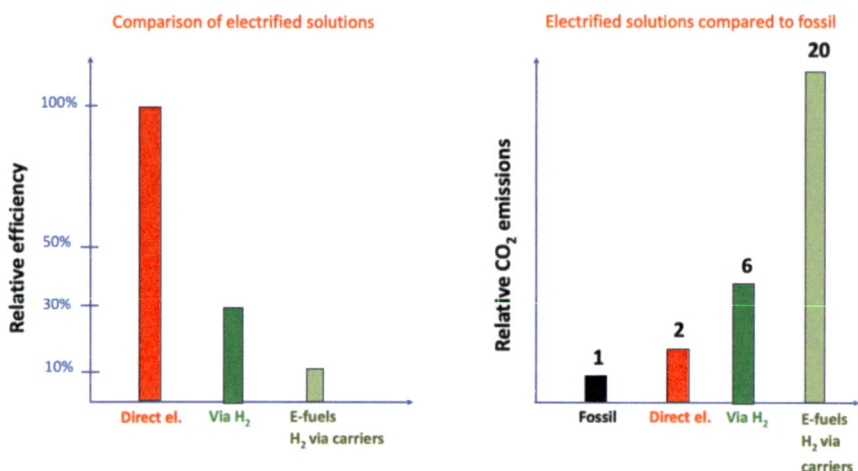

Figure 3.5: Comparison of efficiencies of electrified solutions and consequences for CO2 relative to the fossil when Last-power is coal.

3.7.4. Other energy losses in production of NH3 used as a H2 carrier for fuel cell applications

Air separation (to N2) and compression efficiency:	0.85
Effectiveness in NH3 synthesis (loss, 300–400 bar pressure):	0.8
Efficiency liquefaction (loss, but less than for H2):	0.95
Efficiency transport (liquid, under pressure or cooling):	0.95
Effectiveness decomposition to H2 (in case of fuel cell for electricity production):	0.8
Fuel cell efficiency:	0.6

For the perspective it is important to remember in this context:

- Directly electrified car is ca. 3 times as effective compared to going via H2.
- Directly electrified car is ca. 9 times as effective compared to going via NH3.

3.7.5. Possibilities with the oxyfuel method

The annual global ammonia {14} production is about 240 tonnes/year. Almost all are produced via H2 from natural gas and the catalytic reaction of hydrogen and nitrogen at high temperatures and pressure.

Overall, brown ammonia production from natural gas is energy-intensive, consuming 8 MWh/ton {15} => 1900 TWh, for production of the global amount. This energy amount is mostly due to natural gas which is used as an H2 source and also for combustion/heating purposes. Some smaller shares are electricity for compression/cooling, etc.

Roughly 11 MWh of electricity {16} is needed to produce a ton of ammonia electrolytically. The electricity consumption of a PtA (Power to Ammonia) plant is predominantly attributed to the electrolysis process. Other sources {17} claim slightly more: 10 MWh/ton power need => about 2500 TWh for global transformation to e-NH3. This energy is then supplied as the Last-power.

2500 TWh corresponds to almost all of EU's power (2800 TWh) and about 10% of the global power consumption. This definitively has climate consequences and should be addressed in this book and all other books concerning this issue. We are afraid that we are more or less alone. 1900 TWh of Last-Power means an emission of about 2 Gtons CO_2. In calculations like this, we have to be aware that since the Last-Power equals the time derivative of the power consumption, we can't say that we can calculate the percentage of the total CO_2 emission in this way—for that we need to use the power mix which *emits* about the half CO_2 of the Last-Power.

Difficult to understand? Don't care, very few understand this. Just believe it. (Very few do that as well…)

Nothing wrong with ammonia, we believe that it does a great job of enabling us to eat enough—for many even more than enough—food most days in our lives. What is more disturbing is that now somebody, because there is no carbon in the ammonia molecular structure, wants to use ammonia, e.g., as fuel for transport. But we have written about that elsewhere in the book, so we leave it here. What is wrong is the way ammonia is produced today. By using the oxyfuel method, we may produce really green ammonia. The CO_2 emission may be dramatically reduced. **Figure 3.6** on the next page shows a general outline of an oxyfuel process.

The main advantage of the oxyfuel method is that we avoid the power-demanding capture step in CCS, the H_2 may be separated from the exhaust gas, and the remaining CO_2 along with some pollutants (max 20%) may be stored directly. This makes the CCS much less power-demanding and may be used even in Phase 1 when the Last-Power is coal power {20}.

Another advantage with oxyfuel is that more compact equipment can be applied since N_2 is not present. Also, lower total pressures can be applied for the same reason.

Along with the case shown in Chapter 3.6.1 (gas power plant) {11}, the oxyfuel method has been used in a 300 MW power plant in South Korea since 2009.

R&D on oxyfuel has been going on for decades, but still, there are issues to be solved, perhaps in special according safety; widespread use of pure oxygen needs thorough safety precautions. Besides R&D issues are temperature control, materials, and Solid Oxide Fuel Cells which have integrated separation of O_2 and N_2.

Introducing a new technique on a large scale demands worldwide international cooperation both for still needed R&D and production. Remember that H2 is neither suited for transport nor storage.

Nevertheless, this method also has the big advantage of taking care of surplus energy for wind and sun-power by storing H2.

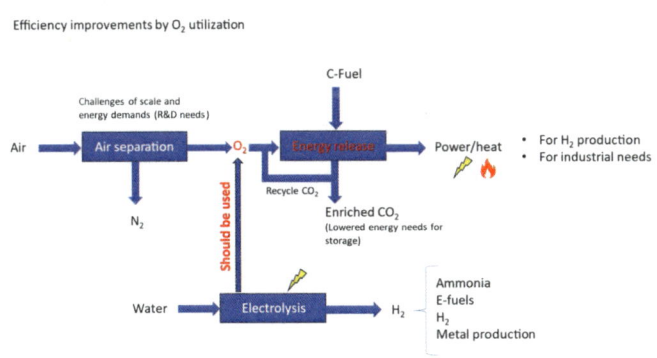

Figure 3.6: Outline of a general oxyfuel process. {18} The technical specifications {19} are found here.

Note: For ammonia production, we need H2, therefore one should use electrolysis of water to get the O2 since that also produces the needed H2. For purposes where H2 is not a wanted product, other ways of producing O2 may be better.

In Chapter 6, we recommend the world to start an immense increase in R&D on 4th generation nuclear power (4GNP). At best, we may mass produce 4GNP plants in about 10 years. However, the oxyfuel method technique may be ready for use long before that. And the investments in oxyfuel technique will never be excessive, so there are no reasons to delay the start of a new "climate adventure".

3.8. Biofuels

3.8.1. Introduction

Biofuel has almost gone from being praised for being "the solution" to hopefully "being able to make a good contribution". The drop in biofuels' status was caused by the recognition of various limitations. A difficult question is the competition with food production. Then ethics kick in and the implementation level is now capped by regulations. Access to enough sustainable raw materials is a challenge. The focus is, therefore, increasingly on the future utilisation of energy in various forms of waste, entering the so-called circular economy.

Thermochemical methods can be developed to convert plastics, organic household waste, building materials, and other industrial waste into energy carriers or fuels. Current raw materials are diverse in physical nature and chemical composition, and the chemistry required to do something with them is largely complex and non-standardised. This makes it more difficult to achieve high efficiency. The practical significance of CO_2 emissions in this area will be limited in the foreseeable future. The use of biofuels is under development in both transport and metal production, and certainly other things.

However, the greatest effect of bio on CO_2 emissions would be obtained anyway by using it to replace coal power.

However, it is now the case that the EU's climate plan includes stepping up bio in aviation and marine transport on a large scale. It is a similarity with H2 and e-fuels that ambitions and objectives are "far off" the realities.

3.8.2. Perspectives and scope

A natural start is to look a little closer at perspectives and scope. The total global biofuel production in 2017 was approx. 970 TWh, of which 623 TWh was ethanol, 284 TWh was conventional FAME (Fatty Acid Methyl Esters) biodiesel, and 61 TWh was so-called HVO (Hydrogenated Vegetable Oils). This is according to the Swedish consulting company Chalmers-Industri-Teknikk AB {21} (CIT). Production of that magnitude covers approx. 3% of the global pool of liquid fuels, which is approx. 31080 TWh. This is mostly first-generation fuels from sugar crops and vegetable oils (agricultural products) for mixing into liquid fuels.

The use of these is "capped" at 7% in the EU regulations (renewables directive), i.e., an upper limit has been set due to the ethics lurking in the background.

Increasing capacity via second-generation advanced fuels is produced either from organic waste or from lignocellulose. The total quantity of advanced liquid biofuels produced in 2016/17 is estimated by CIT to be approx. 27 TWh/year (approx. 3.0 Mm^3/year), disregarding the use of the waste from palm oil production, so-called Palm Fatty Acid Distillate (PFAD). This corresponds to less than 3% of the total biofuel production (3% of the 4% is a small number) and less than 0.1% of the total energy used in transport. CIT has assessed the development of advanced biofuels up to 2030.

In scenario "Low", the total amount in 2023 amounts to approx. 54 TWh. 39 TWh when disregarding PFAD (Palm Fatty Acid Distillate) as raw material. Corresponding estimates for 2030 are up to 104 TWh and 74 TWh. In scenario "High", considered less realistic, it is assumed that all existing plans are realised and that all new and existing facilities produce at full capacity in the planned start year. The total quantity in 2023 is then equivalent to 85 TWh, or 61 TWh without fuel from PFAD as raw material.

In 2030, the amount is 149 TWh and 106 TWh, respectively. This is far below 1% of the total amount of energy used in transport as of today. The significance of global CO_2 emissions will therefore be small.

There are good reasons to believe that there will be (small) contributions from "bio" in the fuel area, but that it cannot be expected in an order of magnitude and speed that means a lot in a climate context. In the organic area, the lowest-hanging fruit has largely already been harvested. However, the technology being developed is relevant to circular economy, i.e., it can contribute to better waste management.

Even with the ambition of only partial success, it will take a long time to develop efficient technology and capacity.

However, further research can contribute to developing new technologies for purification-separation and upgrading to miscellaneous. There are a number of chemical codes that must be cracked. Without those codes being broken, CO_2 emissions can also increase from this area. Perhaps the most important thing is that there may be better solutions to various environmental problems, for example, the utilisation of plastic waste.

But, after all, for climate and CO2 emissions, in our perspective, it would be the very best thing to use "bio" to reduce coal power. It may be an idea to prioritise fuel for air transport as much as possible. But liquid fuel is the hardest substance to optimise.

3.9. Summary of Green H2, E-fuels, and Bio

The time has come to summarise key issues. The energy efficiency for green hydrogen and e-fuels (including ammonia) is approximately 30% and 10% (optimistic), respectively. This is approximately 3 and 10 times less efficient than direct electrification. It can be visualised as green H2 and e-fuels shrinking the exploitable part of the energy system by 70 and 90% respectively. When the Last-power is coal power, the CO2 emission will be approximately 6 times higher for a hydrogen-powered than for a fossil-powered process, while it will be as much as 15–20 times higher for a process powered by e-fuels.

When the Last-power becomes gas power, these ratios are roughly halved. Note: This underlines the necessity that coal power must be phased out before extensive electrification in general.

This means that the use of green hydrogen and e-fuels, regardless of other conditions, will increase CO2 emissions dramatically compared to fossil energy, both when coal power and gas power are the Last-power. We, therefore, preferably should ignore these forms of energy on a large scale until both gas and coal power are phased out in about 30–40 years at the earliest. (*But an immediate start of building 4GNK plants may perhaps reduce this time.*) H2, e-fuels, and bio can only become relevant on a large scale when there is a surplus of low-emission power. And then, these fuels can only be increased so much that one does not have to restart the production of fossil power.

Fossil-powered air and ship traffic can be gradually phased out as the amount of nuclear power increases in *phase 3*. (But at that time, and probably much earlier, it will be much cheaper and simpler to apply 4GNK, at least for ships.) Electrified road traffic can start slowly and increase gradually when gas power has become the Last-power *(Phase 2.)*

Production of biopower or biofuel will never be so large that it has any significant impact on global CO2 emissions. It is doubtful whether it reduces CO2 emissions at all.

For these reasons, we will not focus on the fuels, green hydrogen, e-fuels, and "bio" in this book from now on. On a large scale, as "solutions" to the CO2 problem, these should be forgotten as soon as possible and not taken up again until well into phase 3.

Summary Chapter 3

- Basic data for power (in ACER) is presented and distributed by raw material/sources—types of power.
- Global and European (ACER's) CO2 emissions (distributed by sector) are shown.
- Energy density of energy sources and carriers sets strong guidelines for efficiency and applications (too big, too heavy, etc.)
- Use of Last-power varies in line with the power consumption in ACER and determines the carbon footprint.
- Infill-power is needed to balance unstable power generation. Unstable power must have a plan for Infill-power! There is currently a major shortage of low-carbon Infill-power in ACER.
- Pumped power can contribute to better utilisation of resources and better stabilisation and must be expanded so that the phenomenon of "surplus power" will not exist. New stable nuclear power can contribute in this respect.
- Combustion releases energy by producing H2O and CO2 (energy bottom level). It is, therefore, a paradox that society wants to trust in the use of water and CO2 as resources for energy purposes. Inevitably, and as a direct consequence of the laws of thermodynamics, it requires a really great deal of energy input, thus also explaining the problematically low efficiencies.
- Producing electricity via H2 has an energy efficiency of 30%. That is a waste of energy and is a really "bad deal". Theoretically, a total transition to the hydrogen society shrinks energy to applications by 70%.
- When the Last-power is coal power, a vehicle that consumes 0.3 kWh/mile via green H2 will emit approx. 1 kg CO2/mile, about 6 times more than a fossil car. When gas power becomes the Last-power, the emissions for

"electricity via H2" will be halved relative to coal, and will be approx. 3 times larger than for a fossil car.
- Green H2 may be relevant for niche applications, but not for general use.
- E-fuels (liquid hydrocarbons from H2 and CO2) cause a further 70% loss (because 2 out of 3 H2 return to water), it causes more than 90% loss of power in the production of liquid hydrocarbons.
- Historical dead ends are called solutions and are wrongly called zero emissions!
- These forms of energy (green H2, e-fuels) can only become relevant on a large scale when there is a surplus of emission-free power well into phase 3.
- Zero emissions are the "fake" of all time, but low emissions can perhaps be achieved in phase 3 (in 50 years).
- Production of biopower or biofuel will never be so large that it has any significant impact on global CO2 emissions. The basic capacity from raw materials that can be accepted is not present and efficient production at best is far into the future.
- It is doubtful whether "bio" reduces CO2 emissions at all.
- It is much more important to use the resources to produce food than a fuel with marginal utility value.
- Reasons for coal power being the Last-power are given, and illustrated by **Figure 1** in the preface. The system response for CO2 in case of increased electrification is always determined by the relevant Last-power.

1. S. Giddey, S.P.S. Badwal, A. Kulkarni: *Review of electrochemical ammonia production technologies and materials.*
2. Korean Electric Power Corporation, TRL Technology Readiness Level: (TRL) 8–9, Carbon capture technologies: A review on technology readiness level. Hesamedin Hekmatmehr et.al

4. Time Perspectives

4.1. Future Increased Power Demand

In Norway, there was "suddenly" a long queue of various initiatives that required a lot of power. The queue was so long that there was now talk of an imminent power shortage. This was how the world would be saved. But green?

Electrification of offshore oil/gas platforms is a good example of a measure that leads to a very large increase in power demand. This is about at least 10–20 TWh/year and we have seen even bigger figures. There are gas turbines on the platforms that currently supply power and heat, which are to be shut down in favour of power via cables from shore. Organisations representing oil and gas say, for example, that the gas turbines are inefficient and that exported gas will be used more efficiently where it arrives. But as our calculations in Chap. 2.2.4 shows, that electrification still increases the CO_2 emission by a factor of about 2 and, in fact, probably a lot more.

Besides, offshore turbines can also be made more efficient. Currently, most offshore gas power generators are single-cycle generators with a maximum energy efficiency of about 0.35. These are simpler and demand less maintenance than a combined gas power generator which has an energy efficiency of about 0.55.

But what the real crux of the matter from our side (which never comes up) is that the discussion assumes that the increased power demand that comes with the electrification of platforms has no carbon footprint whatsoever. All use of power in Norway is "marked" zero emissions in today's perception of reality. It is completely surreal and a good example of how the emissions are actually moved to another location and cause the calculation system to fail. The energy balance is forgotten or suppressed. The whole issue is that you cannot take away our surplus power, which we have to use to remove coal power.

On the contrary, coal power will have to increase. The illusion is alive and well. Norway gets the emissions, which we actually send more than double abroad, approved as reduced emissions in the EU's CO_2 accounts. The more emissions Norway "cuts", the more CO_2 there is in the atmosphere. In the world of ethics and the climate, there is a big paradox. Moreover, this wasted electrification will cost many tens of billions of NOK. The cost-benefit principle breaks down.

However, it is perhaps easier when you use "other people's" money. On top of all, the EU has found that the use of gas and nuclear power can now be classified as green in the EU taxonomy, albeit with a set of difficult-to-achieve criteria, including 270 g/kWh. In any case, it provides openings. Is it because they realise that electrification and the lack of Infill-power make this absolutely necessary? In that case, they should be credited for starting to think.

We know that within ACER, it matters little where power is produced and where it is used. So once power is online, it cannot be dedicated to specific purposes. But in practical terms, it is of course an advantage to use the nearest produced power to reduce transmission losses on the network. But this is automatically handled by the power systems.

If we think carefully about this, we can probably dig up several examples of large Norwegian electrification plans. After all, we have cryptocurrency, data centres, and battery factories. Yes, we need enough battery factories, but not now, not until we have phased out coal power. And we can mention transport in the same category. A lot of new power must be unearthed in the next 10 years if all the plans we have seen are to be realised. There will be far more than 10 TWh of new annual demand in Norway just for these planned centres and factories.

This is more than enough to disturb the energy balance. The consumption part of the energy balance increases a lot and must be covered with new power in order for it to come together. It is very un-green to put it nicely.

The crypto-mining and data centres do not replace any emission sources. The calculation for CO_2 only consists of pluses and no minuses. No reduction, only increases. And no one "in the system" reacts. Total brainwashing. Cryptocurrency mining should also be considered green jobs! It is necessary to purchase "renewable energy" and work intensely to maintain the illusion. Everything electrical automatically turns green in the illusion. There probably won't be many jobs either when all the digging is done because these are highly automated things. 'Power rules,' says Roy.

4.2. Reductions in CO2 Emissions Require the Right Action at the Right Time

How well-equipped are we to achieve the planned reductions?

According to today's adopted political objectives, society has very little time to reduce global CO2 emissions. The politicians have given us (or themselves) approx. 7 years to roughly halve emissions. Then we are not only talking about Norway in Europe but about the whole world. The starting point here is, after all, industries that are terribly slow to change, partly because they require access to technologies that have not been fully developed and matured, such as energy storage on a large scale.

In the EU, and especially Germany, there is now a dramatic shortage of pumping power in relation to the installed amount of unstable wind and solar power. Unfortunately, much also indicates that there is a lack of a realistic understanding of what the problem itself entails; and how it must be done. It is not understood at a superior level where energy balances prevail. There is very little evidence that an academic basis has a sufficient impact on what is promoted by measures and plans.

The measures proposed in Norway have, as we have shown in Chap. 2, exactly the opposite effect of what one wants. Most will increase global emissions significantly. One reason for this is "the wrong measures and the wrong sequence at the wrong time". The problem seems to be that those who should take control of this do not have sufficient insight into the problem complex and allow market forces to rule.

Reducing CO2 emissions in the most efficient way requires a plan or strategy. In this chapter, we take a closer look at what the timeline and sequence of measures for extensive future electrification entails. There are some important things to be aware of. Scientifically based choices must be made if emissions are to be successfully reduced. Firstly, one must understand the consequences of emissions of the various measures, and what it entails in terms of consequences for the system as a whole on a macro level.

It requires, among other things, some knowledge of chemistry and an understanding of energy balances and system considerations. Key connections for energy and CO2. How society uses the near future to make itself "wise" is therefore very important. We then consider that we are completely dependent on a good strategic plan in time to manage to reduce emissions on a global level. That plan must take into account three absolutely crucial factors, which measures, the order of the measures, and the scope. We will try to explain that in this chapter.

4.3. The Extent of the Change We are Going Through

In this book, we stick to the close playground that includes the EU and the energy market ACER, in which Norway is involved. We can take a closer look at some figures that put various measures and their order in a quantitative perspective. What is to be replaced (coal, oil, gas) plays a fairly large role. In this book, we have probably indicated slightly differently how long the individual phases will last, depending on the premises in question. **Table 4.1** provides a sad summary.

We remind you that phase 1 lasts until coal power is phased out, phase 2 until gas power is phased out. In phase 3, we are in a low-emission society.

Best case	Likely based on existing plans	Optimistic hope
Phase 1	10 years	Eternal	15–30 years
Phase 2	20 years	Don't even enter it: 0	20–60 years
Phase 3	Eternal	Don't even enter it: 0	Eternal

Table 4.1: Duration of the individual phases.

Notice, we have defined phase 2 so that it lasts until gas power is phased out. The idea has been that then all other fossil energy will also be phased out. It is not necessarily correct, but we simplify here so that phase 2 lasts until both gas power is phased out and land transport is electrified. This will, of course, result in a too short duration of phase 2 because the use of fossil energy in heating, industry, air, and ocean transport, etc. will not yet be phased out. We remind you here that in phase 2 the CO_2 emissions from a fossil and the corresponding electrified process are usually quite similar. Therefore, it is not very important when in phase 2 the electrification takes place.

What must be replaced with new renewables from the "major power sources" in Europe are coal power (approx. 663 TWh) and gas power (approx. 710 TWh), according to the IEA (2019), the last normal year before the Corona epidemic. The two types of power which are relevant for the duration of phases 1 and 2. In addition, we have transport which requires an estimated 1250 TWh of power to replace 2500 TWh of oil energy. More so when the transport is electrified directly using batteries.

Altogether, this will require approx. 2,600 TWh. When using hydrogen as an energy carrier and fuel cells in transport, this will increase to approx. 5,000 TWh, and when using e-fuels/ammonia to approx. 12,000 TWh.

In the 5 years from 2015 to 2019, again according to data from the IEA, an average of approx. 45 TWh of new renewable power per year was produced. We have used an optimistic 50 TWh in our following assessments, although it is more likely that this number will decrease rather than increase as Germany has now experienced problems with the stability of its electricity supply and must/should develop more pumped power before it is appropriate to develop more wind and solar power.

Germany has been the driving force in the development of emission-free power. (And, unfortunately, also in the phasing out of nuclear power...)

The order in which you choose to phase out is important, crucial, in fact. **Figure 4.1** shows that we can phase out coal-fired power in approximately 15 years if it is prioritised. From **Figure 4.1,** we can also see: Phasing out gas power in phase 2 will require a further 12 years. In the time after 27 years from now, oil energy can be replaced with electrified land transport. After approx. 52 years, coal and gas power have been phased out and land transport electrified. Translated into years, it will be in approx. 2075. Prioritised phasing out of coal power produces the lowest total CO2 emissions.

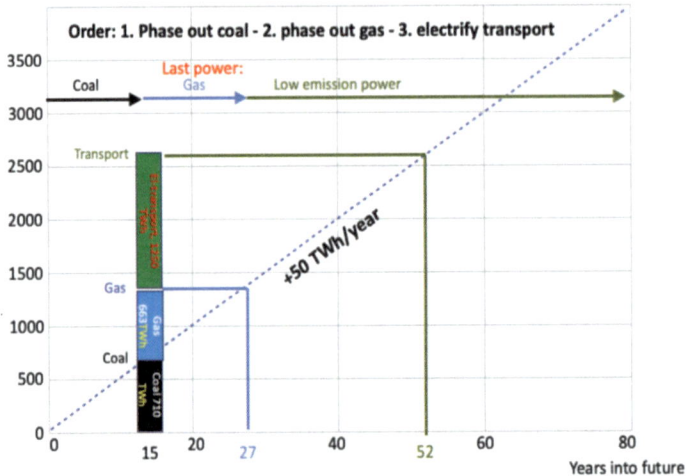

Figure 4.1: Use of new renewables for prioritised phasing out of coal before gas and then transport.

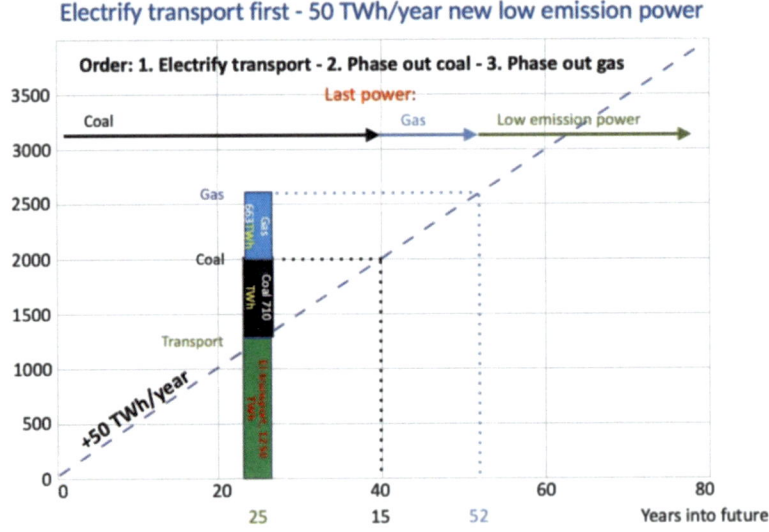

Figure 4.2: Use of new renewables for prioritised phasing out of oil energy in transport with direct electrification, before coal power and finally gas power

Figure 4.2 shows what happens if the current practice of prioritising the electrification of land transport is used as a basis. Based on the same assumption of 50 TWh of new renewables annually, it takes 25 years to replace oil energy in land transport. It will take another 15 years to replace coal power, i.e., 40 years from today. It will be approx. year 2060 before coal power is phased out and 2075 before gas power is also phased out.

Table 4.2 CO_2 emissions depending upon order of phasing out

Priority and emissions		CO_2 emissions [fossil cars]	CO_2 emissions [electric cars]	Total	Lastpower type
Phasing out coal power before electrifying transport					
Year 0 - 10	[Gtons]	21,4	0	21,4	Coal power
Year 10 - 40	[Gtons]	32,1	32,1	64,3	Gas power
Total	[Gtons]	53,6	32,1	85,7	
Electrifying transport before phasing out coal power					
Year 0 - 30	[Gtons]	32,1	64,3	96,4	Coal power
Year 30 - 40	[Gtons]	0	42,9	42,9	Coal power
Total	[Gtons]	32,1	107,2	139,3	

Premises for **Table 4.2**:

- When the Last-power is coal power, electric cars globally emit twice as much CO2 as fossil cars.
- When gas power is the Last-power, electric and fossil cars emit the same amount of CO2.
- Gas power is always available.

Table 4.2 shows how large the CO2 emissions are from fossil-fuel cars, electric cars and the sum of these. The total emissions are highly dependent on which is prioritised first of
1: Phasing out of coal power, or
2: Electrification of land transport.

The fact that the emissions from land transport in the latter case become greater when land transport is electrified, is largely due to the fact that the emissions from electric cars are twice that of fossil cars when coal power is the Last-power. It is assumed that all new emission-free power, 50 TWh per year, is used only for these two purposes.

The consequence of prioritised phasing out of coal power versus prioritised electrifying land transport is shown in **Figure 4.3**. The data for **Figure 4.3** is shown in **Table 4.2**. In that table, it is assumed that fossil fuel land transport starts with a consumption of 3,000 TWh, which is reduced to 0 within 30 years. For that, you only need 1500 TWh of electric power because the energy efficiency of electric cars is about twice as high as that of fossil cars. Furthermore, it is expected that 500 TWh of coal will be phased out within 10 years. In reality, the fossil fuel land transport today uses about 2500 TWh and there is around 700 TWh of coal power that must be phased out.

It is emphasised that this is of course not a very realistic model, but the result nevertheless shows that it is important to prioritise the phasing out of coal power before electrification.

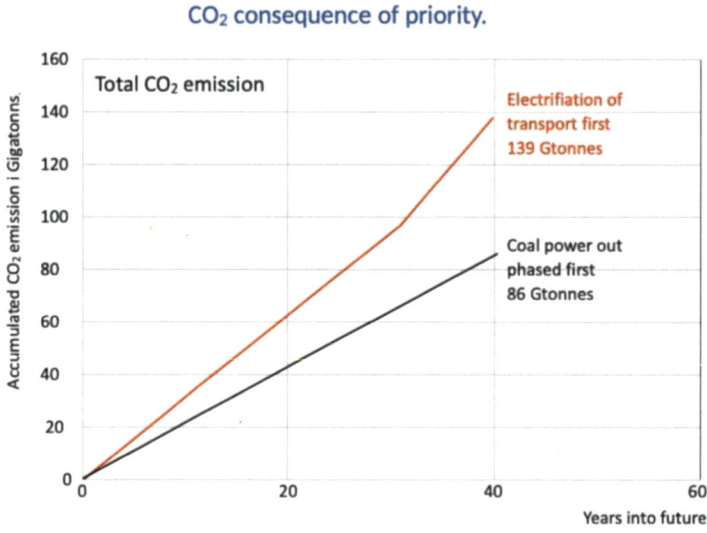

Figure 4.3: Accumulated CO2 emissions over time as a result of different prioritisation of the phasing out of 3000 TWh fossil fuel traffic to 1500 TWh electrified land transport and 500 TWh coal power.

Although we boasted in Chapter 3.5.2.8 that we had carried out a cruel "double kill" on hydrogen and e-fuels for phases 1 and 2, we cannot resist the temptation to show what happens if the focus is on these energy types. It is illustrated in **Figure 4.4**, which compares how long it will take to electrify transport for the cases "direct", "H2" and "e-fuels". As previously shown in

Figure 4.2, it takes 25 years to replace oil energy with direct electrified transport. With "electricity to electricity via H2", it will take 75 years and with e-fuels, it will take 240 years.

With H2, it will be close to the year 2100 and with e-fuels, the year 2260 before land transport is electrified and you can start phasing out coal power. Since we are only looking at the time it takes for out phasing, it does not matter what the status of coal power and gas power is. CO2 emissions will, of course, increase dramatically if this is done before coal power and gas power are phased out.

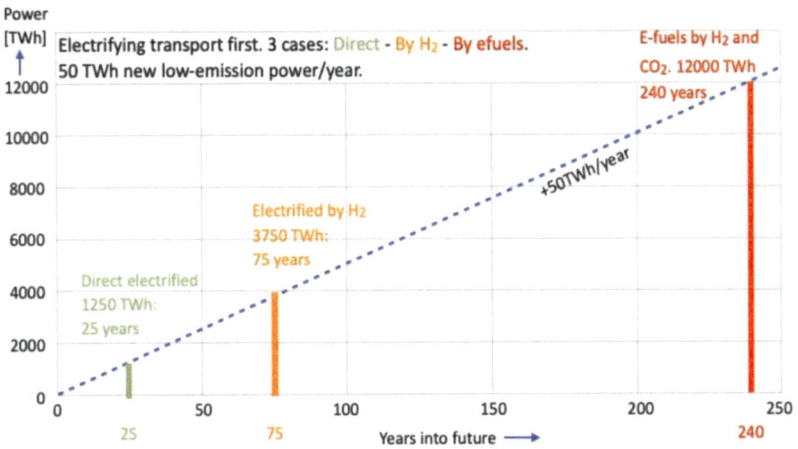

Figure 4.4: Prioritised phasing out of oil energy with, direct electrification, via H2, via e-fuels.

If we choose to invest in ammonia, which has practical advantages (easier to liquefy) than hydrogen, the same amount of power will be used for e-fuels, at least 10,000 TWh.

These are very simple relationships, and one has to ask oneself: Why is this not understood by the governing bodies neither within the EU nor Norway? Are there too many and too strong forces that want to profit grossly from this idiocy? Where are H. C. Andersen's old clothes? All professionals in this area must understand this. Do political views, illusions, and financial incentives have more power than professional knowledge? 'Illusions are blind,' says Roy.

If we choose to use the power to electrify transport, there will be less power to replace coal power. That's how it is! We know that, and it is so obvious that everyone should know it. In addition, some countries have decided to move away from nuclear power, which accounts for as large a share as approx. 26% of the EU's total power production of 3200 TWh, i.e., approx. 650 TWh. We will see how it develops, but it is a bright spot that the EU has now finally opened its eyes to the fact that nuclear power is necessary to be able to meet the emission targets. Nuclear power is necessary when we look at the challenges we face. **Table 4.2** and **Figures 4.1** to **4.4** are all based on the nuclear power being kept constant.

What happens to nuclear power is important for the time course indicated in figures 4.1, 4.2, and 4.4. In this perspective, it is quite obvious that the development of more nuclear power should/must start immediately. In any case, efforts to prepare 4th generation nuclear power must be intensified.

If CO_2 reductions are a priority, nuclear power must not only be retained but greatly increased as soon as possible.

The sum of what is to be replaced and what is added due to the electrification of land transport is more than 3,000 TWh. At least we are talking about a doubling of current power production in Europe in the very extensive total restructuring. The 2030 targets almost tell that it will happen overnight to establish such large amounts of new renewable energy. In Norway, it is now suggested that it may take over 10 years just to adjust the bottlenecks in transmission capacity in the supply network.

It doesn't sound promising; a huge effort must also be made to increase the Infill-power with pumped power plants and/or hydrogen produced, as described in Chap. 3.4.2, so that all the new wind and solar power can be used in an appropriate way. But, in a way, it's also a bit positive since society gets more time to think about it. If the politicians become more interested in realities, that's a good thing.

This means that phase 1 may last from 10 years at best until much longer. The ability to prioritise in practice is decisive. An important prerequisite for society to be successful in this phase is that the resources are used primarily to develop low-emission power together with necessary Infill-power for the current amount of wind and solar power. The second condition is that we do not carry out unnecessary new electrifications. We cannot increase the power requirement with all the "measures" that are on the table and are being pushed forward. On the contrary, we must reduce power consumption through extensive power efficiency measures.

Replacing coal power is, therefore, a clear first priority on behalf of the climate. In order to be able to do this within a reasonable time, we must basically put aside the idea of hydrogen and e-fuel production (Chapters 3.6 and 3.7). These thoughts must remain well hidden until the end of phase 2, i.e., for approx. 50 years.

You can also look at this from a slightly different perspective. For a given amount of CO_2, the consequence is least for coal power in the form of the number of TWh that is lost (must be replaced) when it is phased out. If you reduce the gas power to achieve the same amount of reduced CO_2, you will lose twice as much power. This means that the wisest thing, also in that perspective, is to focus on coal power. It has the least negative consequences for the power system. It is simply the best solution for society.

So, the matter is really crystal clear: *The maximum reduction of CO_2 emissions in the coming years requires no new unnecessary electrifications, maximum effort on the construction of nuclear power plants and the necessary pumped power plants and/or hydrogen produced as described in Chap. 3.7.5.*

If one follows this plan, it may be possible to remove coal power by 2035. In the meantime, CO_2 is spewing out from the Chinese, Indian, American, and European…coal power plants. We feel quite strongly that many people need to realise what the situation really is. But we, in Europe, will be able to enjoy the fact that we have done our part and got a nice and clean Europe that only emits a little CO_2 from cars, low-emitting gas power plants, and maybe a little more. If the EU does as we suggest.

And a small plus: The 663 TWh of coal-fired power (2019) that can be removed, amounts to approx. 30% of the EU's CO_2 emissions, and we may be able to achieve that in 10–15 years. Great! And we have done it in the cheapest way!

Many may think this is bad in relation to the plans for a 50% CO_2 reduction by 2030, but our plan has the significant advantage that it is realistic and will work.

4.4. The Gaps in Society's Strategy

The big gap is that the phasing out of coal power, with the highest emission intensity, is not a priority. The power must be used for everything else. What is prioritised is the electrification of transport, data centres, cryptocurrency mining, and oil/gas platforms; yes, the whole long list. Phasing out coal power has never been on that list. Society does not see the need to take into account the conditions within the three phases. Much is left to the market. The power is used for the wrong purpose and has a completely wrong consequence on CO_2 emissions. 'They go straight to heaven,' says Roy. 'Literally.'

In Norway, we are overly concerned with electrifying transport. But, in this book, we have clearly shown that in the current phase, it only leads to increased global CO_2 emissions. 'We shit in the neighbour's garden,' says Roy. Electrifying transport is completely unnecessary for the time being. It even about doubles transport's global CO_2 emissions. We have to get to phase 2 where natural gas is the Last-power before it makes any sense to start with that type of electrification. 'Then I bought myself an electric car 40 years too early,' says Roy.

There is a high probability that the estimated 500 TWh of new renewable energy in the coming 10-year period will not be used to replace any of the fossil energy but to supplement it. There is no one who really controls this. The only "control" is the increase of the CO_2 quotas. So far that has had a limited impact. The website of the German Fraunhofer Institute for Solar Energy shows that from 2002 to 2016, the share of renewables in the German power system increased from 2% to over 50%, but coal power remained stable throughout the period. You trust the market and there, the main focus is on increasing profits in the form of cash.

There will be a battle for power for various purposes. It is not the case that 500 TWh renewables can simply be phased in straight away. At the same time, it requires large amounts of Infill-power, which today is natural gas, hydropower, but also to a certain extent coal power. When, in 5–10 years' time, we have established 4th generation nuclear power, they will also have good enough dynamic properties to function as Infill-power.

But it is important that the Infill-power also has the option of storing surplus power; none of the power types mentioned here have that option, so normally, you should also establish pumping power where it is appropriate and/or hydrogen produced as described in Chap. 3.7.5.

If we do not take the problem of Infill-power seriously, it is predominantly likely that we will end up in a situation where increased renewables require increased fossil fuels.

There is also a gap in society's strategy—they do not have a clear picture of how much new renewable energy we can generate. The power needs that are predicted now seem to come as a surprise to politicians. And few/no politicians are concerned with nuclear power, which will be absolutely necessary to be able to approach even the least ambitious targets.

In order to achieve the agreed emission targets, a very large amount of power must be generated by 2030 and 2050. The question is, where will all this energy come from? Onshore wind power faces strong opposition in large parts of Europe. In Norway too, it has reached a level where there is resistance both among the population and therefore also politically. It is claimed that battery factories will be able to claim approx. 3 TWh annually. Several of the measures are in this order of magnitude, or significantly higher.

If we see this in relation to what the Norwegian Frøya wind farm can generate, which is approx. 0.2 TWh per year, means that one battery factory will require all the energy from 15 such wind farms.

Electrification of offshore platforms is estimated to consume power in the order of 15 TWh per year. That "measure" will, therefore, need 75 wind farms like Frøya. This illustrates well the scope we are talking about.

A little more hydropower can perhaps be pushed out with more efficient turbines and a little increase in the maximum filling of some reservoirs, but not much in the grand scheme of things. Offshore wind is being worked on but there is little indication that it will make a significant contribution in the first 10 years. Construction of nuclear power will be much more efficient, but even for these, it will take at least 5–10 years before the first 4th generation nuclear power plants can be ready for production.

4.5. Reduced Standard of Life, but Better Standard of Living?

An important point we have not included here: It is obvious that the fight against the climate threat will be demanding. It is, therefore, an important political task to prepare people for that fact. It can be simple things such as greatly reduced holiday travel by plane, higher taxes and duties…simply put, reduced standard of living. The motivation for such a development must be that, through a concerted effort to reduce consumption, we can have opportunities for an equal fight against climate change.

We believe people will eventually understand this and return to a lifestyle we had a few decades ago. And perhaps we have to work more purposefully so that the reduced standard of living in terms of money and goods is compensated with a better standard of living.

This reduced activity will challenge our economic system with its built-in requirement: Steady growth. But this may partly be compensated for by increased activity with climate-friendly measures such as the development of pumped and nuclear power, energy efficiency, measures, and possibly the hydrogen produced by the oxyfuel technique as described in Chap. 3.7.5.

Today, we see the consequences of power shortages with sharp increases in prices and growing disdain for politicians. Both parts are enough to fear for the future. It turns out that everything is in a very sensitive equilibrium and even small changes *may* have large and, for society, unimaginable consequences. If there is no professional basis and anchoring among "ordinary people", this will not go well.

Summary Chapter 4

- There are plans for an extremely large increase in electricity consumption in the community. There is a queue to get power! Where will all this power come from? Today (Phase 1), it must come from coal power. (Last-power).
- We have to generate new electricity before we can use it!
- Measures must come at the right time. Wrong prioritisation of measures => large extra CO2 emissions.
- Electrification must wait until coal power is phased out.
- One must invest in nuclear power for stable power and must have sufficient Infill-power available for any new unreliable wind-solar power. Nuclear power will reduce the need for Infill-power.
- Development of pumping power and the hydrogen produced by the oxyfuel technique as described in Chap. 3.7.5 must be intensified. Market forces have clearly shown that it does not work for this.

- The scope of the problem indicates that Europe/ACER needs approx. 2,600 TWh of "new power" to replace coal/gas power and electrify land traffic with direct electricity. If this is done entirely with H2 or alternatively e-fuels, approx. 7,000/20,000 TWh is needed respectively.
- The annual increase in emission-free power has been 45–50 TWh in the last 5 years, far lower than the indicated need.
- Priority phasing out of coal can be done within 10–15 years (Phase 1). Then phasing out gas power (Phase 2). Gas power cannot be phased out until sufficient new stable power is available. (Nuclear power, contribution from pumped power, and the hydrogen produced by the oxyfuel technique as described in Chap. 3.7.5 must be intensified.)

5. About Realism and Feasibility

5.1. The Challenges Quantified in the Big Picture

5.1.1. Random and unrealistic objectives

According to the UN's current targets: {22}

2030: To keep global warming to 1.5 degrees, countries must cut emissions by ca. 42%.

2050: The transition to net-zero emissions must be fully complete.

When we wrote our "Electrification: Carbon Footprint and Emissions" in June 2020, we had an optimistic hope that phase 3 could be more or less finished by about 2070. UN's targets seem very unrealistic to us and if they don't understand the principles in this book, they haven't read it yet, we know that their targets are impossible to reach.

Since 2020, we have experienced that local targets, like Norway's, apparently have been taken out of thin air, and they only go one way—to more and more unrealistic levels. Without any indication that the targets are possible, they can be adjusted from a 50% to 60% reduction by 2030, the most eager want 80%.

There is nothing to suggest that this is close to being possible because almost all the measures increase global CO_2 emissions. Most of the "solutions" highlighted require more power, a lot of power, and coal power is not being phased out, it is likely to increase globally.

5.1.2. Global perspective

The development of global CO2 emissions 1940–2023 is shown in fig. 5.1 on the next page. The figure clearly shows the effect of the pandemic 2020–2022 and that the pandemic only caused a pause in the increase in global CO2 emissions. It says something about how dramatic the measures required are if the goal is to be achieved. China alone accounts for over 10 Giga-tons of the emissions. They are still building new coal-fired power but claim that they will achieve net-zero emissions in 2060, i.e., become carbon neutral. It is perhaps as credible as the rest of the world's unrealistic plans, or perhaps we should rather call it the faith and hope of the West.

The big problem is the dependence on fossil power. Today, coal, oil, and gas make up almost 85% of primary energy globally. The rest is covered by nuclear power, hydropower, and other renewables. Coal alone makes up almost 30% of the entire energy mix, approximately 90% of the coal is used for power/heat production. Many countries have built up an energy system based on the resources they have themselves.

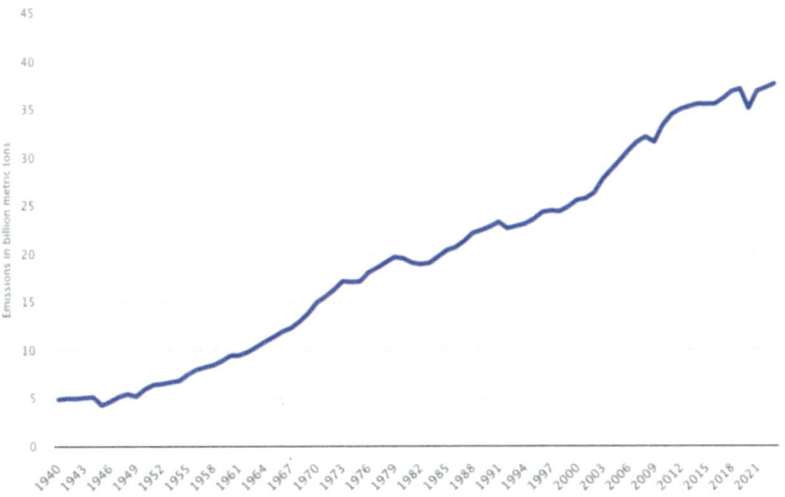

Figure 5.1: From Statista: {23} Development of global CO2 emissions 1940–2023
82/83 Statista

Globally, coal power accounts for approximately 10,000 TWh annually, while gas and hydropower account for 6,000 and 4,000 TWh respectively. When coal has approx. twice the CO2 footprint of natural gas, the carbon footprint of electricity is to a very large extent determined by the amount of coal power in the system. In addition, coal-fired power plants are less efficient than gas-fired power plants. That's why we say coal must go. In China, coal dominates even more, they alone have a share of the global CO2 emission of more than 25%! They have some hydropower, but all the other types of power are small, only a few per cent of the total.

Almost 90% of the oil is used for transport. Among other things because it has superior properties in the form of high energy density. It's nice to know that you'll get to your destination when flying long distances. Liquid fuels can be easily stored, for example, in a Coke bottle, but neither electricity nor hydrogen can do that. These extremely simple but powerful properties are hard to beat. Everything else becomes more expensive, more demanding and complicated.

Emissions of CO2 from power/heat production on our planet are approx. 35% higher than from transport (oil-based). The high emission level comes from coal's high CO2 intensity (Coal = 2, Oil = 1.5, Natural gas = 1, relatively speaking). It is obvious that coal must be phased out before electrification. The actual cause of the problem needs to be tackled first. When one voluntarily jumps over to the energy chain, which is dominated by coal power, by electrifying, it necessarily has a large "CO2 consequence".

This was clarified in the presentation we gave to the Norwegian Ministry of Oil and Energy (OED) during a virtual meeting in May 2020.

5.2. CCS on a Large Scale

A small preliminary comment: In Chapter 3.7.5, we showed an opportunity to improve the CCS system by using the oxyfuel method to enrich the CO2 concentrations in the fuel gases, thus avoiding the capture step. This chapter shows CCS technologies of today does not seem to be able to "save the world". But by applying the oxyfuel method, if it can be realised, it will be dramatically much better because the entire "Capture phase" can be avoided. Keep that in mind when reading this chapter.

5.2.1. Introduction

It has now been about 15 years since the capture and storage of CO2 was supposed to save the world. Some baits are irresistible. It is easy to grab the first shot when you give others a noble agenda. Then it spreads easily. At the time, there was already a great rush to capture the Earth's CO2, and it was the Earth's doom if it was not carried out within a very short time. We had no time to lose. The rhetoric was almost hysterical. It actually spread quite a bit of anxiety. An illusion built up in many circles that it was easy to do, and that this was the technology of the future that we will develop and live by in the future.

"Some" wrote reports that it would create thousands of jobs. The politicians got stuck and the pressure increased. The world would be completely dependent on this technology. The whole world had to adopt it. There were a lot of big words. This repeats itself at regular intervals.

5.2.2. What is the status now?

There are expectations linked to the Norwegian "Longship" {24} project and CO_2 capture from the case of cement production and the Hafslund {25} project utilising the energy from a waste incineration plant. The principle is explained in Chapter 5.2.5.

Now we have got numbers for the use of power (private communication) in the "Hafslund" project. The numbers show that when the Last-power is coal power, the CCS process emits roughly the same amount of CO_2 as is captured (1 kg CO_2/kWh emitted for 1 kWh/kg CO_2 captured). The reason why the project leaders have not observed this dramatic fact, probably is the same as for all cases like this: They don't understand the CO_2 footprint of the Last-power. In the CCS project: {26} "Norwegian Ministry of Petroleum and Energy, Meld. St. 33 (2019–2020) Report to the Storting (white paper), Longship—Carbon capture and storage", on page 14, you find the sentence: "The power sector can also cut emissions by switching to renewable energy sources".

We have checked a lot of reports from this project but this is the only report which mentions this issue at all. The quoted sentence tells: They don't understand, or want to understand, that power can't be delegated (See Chap. 5.3.1.), and/or they don't understand, or want to understand, the concept of Last-power (See Chap. 3.3).

Within the EU, the enthusiasm for CCS has obviously cooled somewhat; under "Report from the Commission to the European Parliament and the Council" dated 26 October 2021, we find: "Only Norway declared CCS activities". We are still the most beautiful and clever students in the class!

CCS has moved down on the scale of urgency as certain realities sink in. We may be able to say that the technology was nowhere as ready as "someone" claimed. Because the realities of Last-power were not recognised, and people could not see the big picture, the positive climate effects of CCS were only an illusion! At the time, we only had a few years left, "before it was too late for civilisation as we know it today". By the way, it was a rhetoric that goes all the way back to the 70s. It was like seeing the rise of a new religion where CCS was the technological path to salvation. It grew into its own item on the state budget and is still there. "Some" succeeded!

With such noble motives and such high pressure, it is difficult for politicians to resist. And, as you know, they have large money bags which are easy to drool over. There was so much that was unclear and not assessed.

This technology has been given far more space than it deserves from a consideration of the technology's own premises. It has actually been elevated to "political technology", and then, there is a completely different game taking place, which lives its own life with its own rules.

5.2.3. Maturity of the technology

Another item is the actual maturity of the technology and when it is really ready to be used on a large scale (industrially). The development time for chemical processes with acceptable efficiency is often several decades. Then we are talking about conditions such as lifespan and energy efficiency. And when it comes to CCS, we are talking about technology that must be linked to emissions where the framework conditions are very different. It is, therefore, difficult to envision standardised facilities.

Usually, this must be taken in small steps from the laboratory to a gradually larger scale via so-called pilots. Scale-ups are normally very risky. That's when big problems often arise, costs run up and time flies. However, we are in a situation where there is great pressure to "build large facilities now". Then you easily end up in a dilemma, but it might release a lot of public money. 'An obvious motive,' says Roy. The big risk that comes with taking shortcuts to a scaled-up process is one the taxpayers have to take.

There is no doubt that there is much that may be researched here, but there is far greater doubt as to whether the technology can be built to the degree of maturity that is required. There is even greater doubt as to whether it is ready to be used by many. Has no one asked the question of how long it will and should take? The answer is: Not really!

5.2.4. The Realism of CCS

There are undoubtedly many in the system who put their trust in CCS. The question is whether there is a good reason for it. Here, we would like to say that the thermodynamics and energy-consuming operations which follow, the so-called "energy chain", have been largely overlooked. The degree of industrial reason is not obvious but coercion and scapegoating have an effect and a cost. Little is said about the fact that operating CCS requires a lot of energy, both heat and power. Chemical capture involves cooling amine absorbents to the capture temperature and heating them to release CO_2. Then CO_2 in gaseous form must be cooled to get it into liquid form.

It can then be transported, is temporarily stored and prepared for compression and injection. When this is connected to a power plant, this will produce less energy for other purposes. But CCS in connection with a thermal power plant has the advantage that you get the heat cheaply. Then the question becomes: What percentage of the electricity is used?

CCS must necessarily be done globally on a large scale to have any meaning, the realism is so-so.

Another factor is that if half of the global CO_2 emissions are to be taken with CCS, we must capture 16 Gtons of CO_2 a year. Large emission sources such as a refinery can emit in the order of 1 Mtons a year. Then the calculation is that it will require 16,000 CCS facilities at such large emission points. However, most emission points are much smaller than that. Let's say that we base the calculation on an emission point of the order of 100,000 tons of CO_2 per year, which is also quite large. Then you suddenly have to have a whopping 160,000 plants. This is not realistic. For this to make sense, it must also be both simple and cheap. Everything indicates that it is neither. And most emission points are much less than 100,000 tons of CO_2 a year. The smaller the emission points, the more energy you have to use "per CO_2".

Back to energy use and estimates for the order of magnitude. At an emission point/facility, energy is used to separate CO_2 from the other gases in the exhaust stream, for transport by pipes or ships, and under high pressure for injection to a storage location. It is the capture step that is particularly energy-intensive. It is slow chemistry, therefore the CCS plant is large and inefficient, thus also very expensive.

On large existing industrial facilities, such as power plants, CCS must be retrofitted. It leads to a formidable "punishment". Studies at highly recognised universities have quantified the "energy penalty" of retrofitting CCS to power generation facilities. Researchers at Imperial College London estimate the "research penalty" to be 20% ("Carbon capture technology: future fossil fuel use and mitigating climate change", Nov 2010). Researchers at Harvard University and the Massachusetts Institute of Technology (MIT) claim that it will range from 11%, which is the theoretical minimum, and up to 40%. 29% was considered a realistic level.

Theoretical minimums are never achievable ("The energy penalty of post-combustion CO2 capture and storage", Jan 2009). Loss of power/energy on this scale is very high. The "penalty" must be paid by burning more raw material to maintain power production or possibly reduce power production. According to Harvard and MIT, if implemented in US coal power plants, it would require increased consumption of 400–600 Mtons of coal per year.

5.2.5. Can CCS be used for anything?

To the question of whether CCS can be used for anything, the answer is that it can be used for increased oil extraction, so-called EOR because here CCS is a "business case". In that context, it naturally increases CO2 emissions. It involves, for example, getting the last splashes out of oil fields. What remains after the field is emptied is more difficult to get out than the first splash.

Along with the oil, there is also some natural gas and often CO2. The gas is first separated from the oil. The CO2 can then be separated from the gas by chemically absorbing the CO2 in amine-based solutions. This requires a temperature that is favourable for complexing the CO2 and the amine. It is an equilibrium situation. You need a temperature that is low enough for good equilibrium, but at the same time as high as possible so that it does not go too slowly. When a proportion of CO2 is "captured", the temperature of the amine mixture must be increased to a level where CO2 is released and the amine is regenerated. Full regeneration is the goal so that the capacity does not fall.

This is the big challenge. It can be slow; it requires a lot of energy. This means that the facilities can become extremely large. How much CO2 can be captured depends on the starting concentration. It is beneficial with a high CO2 concentration. The lower the CO2 concentration becomes, the more difficult the capture is. Perhaps you manage to catch 60–80%.

This is the very technology you depend on to achieve all the hairy emission targets. It should have been included in the chapter on "The most dangerous illusions". That question is nevertheless: How much less will the net of released CO2 be and at what price? That is, what will be the difference between the amount of CO2 we capture and the amount of CO2 released from the extra coal; or gas power that must be produced to provide the extra electricity for that capture?

We would have liked to come up with a clear figure here, but no one has calculated this, there are no figures for this. And we have no experience that can give us clear answers.

What is clear is that the capture and storage of various sources, which ultimately end up in a *depot*, lead to a quantifiable amount of x tons of deposited CO2. The question is how much CO2 was emitted to get x there.

What is not quantified is how much global CO2 is emitted due to metal production, the construction of large facilities, pipes, ships, equipment, production of chemicals. And, in addition, the production and operation of the infrastructure. Much of this will also be increased where the Last-power has a meaning. What is crystal clear is that the real number of net reduced CO2 in the atmosphere is much smaller than x. If a global infrastructure is to be built quickly, it is likely that net emissions will also be greater than X, i.e., that more CO2 will be emitted than is deposited. In any case, it will be a very bad deal.

A credible total account must be in place before CCS can be "trusted"! However, the interest in such an accounting with correct pluses and correct minuses looks weak since it would shake the illusions.

Bottom line: CCS should not be expanded until coal power is phased out. And even then, it will be bad business; it will be much more efficient and safer to use the resources for building nuclear power plants. CCS is unlikely to be an effective climate tool until the climate problem is close to being resolved. But CCS may perhaps shorten the transition period between phase 2 and phase 3.

5.2.6. CCS and HSE

5.2.6.1. Chemicals and environment

Another issue is how environmentally friendly CCS really is. Not many people focus on that side of the matter. Often, so-called amines are highlighted as the most promising, so-called liquid absorbents. There are compounds that contain a lot of nitrogen. These must also be produced, and in large quantities.

In the end, they will become special waste that must be incinerated, and then it must be ensured that NOx, NH3, and other components are neither formed nor released. Because that will not be allowed. These amines are actually produced from natural gas. Ethanolamine, for example, is produced from ethylene oxide and ammonia. Ammonia is produced from natural gas.

Ethylene oxide from ethylene and chlorine gas. Ethylene from natural gas by energy-intensive "steam cracking". As we saw in Chapter 3.7.1, the production of ammonia requires large amounts of electricity. It is difficult to escape the fossil world. Why don't such important things come to light?

There is a bad culture of openness about this today. When you drive on in the correct bubble, you can ignore the unpleasant aspects of the matter. The end sanctifies the means to such an extent that uncriticalness becomes a dominant culture.

5.2.6.2. The eternal perspective and CO2 leaks

The purpose of CCS is to store huge amounts of CO2 in underground storage. In fact, we are talking about a large proportion of the existing total amount of CO2, for it to be able to influence the temperature here on the planet. That's the theory. These storage places for CO2 can be located under the sea, such as in drained oil/gas fields, or under land in suitable structures.

There are a couple of concerns. There will always be a risk of leaks. CO2 is stored under pressure and regardless of the cause, natural or man-made, there will be opportunities for CO2 to leak out. On land, this means that CO2 will displace the air. This leads to suffocation for those who are in the "CO2 cloud". It is known that it is not good HSE for either people or wildlife. If a large leak occurs in the sea, this can become very acidic and the consequence is that the ecosystems can be destroyed, nor is it good HSE from nature's point of view.

5.2.7. Other barriers and limitations to CCS

Resource use is an obvious problem for CCS from a sustainability perspective. Most people have probably understood that capturing and handling CO2 requires a lot of energy. The consequence is a high consumption of resources. When it also does not produce marketable products, it goes without saying that the economy is poor. Everything must be pumped down into the underworld to stay there. Norway is aiming to become Europe's carbon waste depot.

There is a lot of ethics at the bottom of the CCS problem. When a large proportion of the world's population lives in energy poverty, can energy prices be increased and rather use the available energy on CO2 capture? Until then, CCS will use more of the resources that we should not use. This is in conflict with good sustainability in several ways. 'Eye patches work,' says Roy.

Society emphasises driving this forward based on pure economic thinking, without understanding the physical and chemical realities involved. The result is a very unfortunate situation where lots of money is spent on very little or no outcome.

Implementation is difficult. Very hypothetical, if very few use it, then those who do use it, will have a disadvantage. Prices must be artificially kept up and controlled by the EU authorities. There is an end to the free market and healthy competition. This is where the carbon tax will make miracles and "force" the world to act according to its plans, i.e., adopt CCS. The carbon tax is dealt with in a separate Chapter 7.2.

If we look at Norway, already after the Mongstad refinery scandal, i.e. the cancelled CCS moon landing it is clear that this was extremely expensive technology. Really, really expensive. And when the goal is that it should—no, must—be used all over the world to capture large shares of the world's emissions, then it is a really bad starting point. The alarm bells are ringing for some, but no one is able to break through the illusions. Thus, the development continues as the years go by. Now it is the "Longship" project that counts. I guess it's the politicians' way of making everyone happy. Popularity and cash flows override all other considerations!

5.2.8. Capture of CO2 directly from the air?

Direct Air Capture (DAC) is a proposed method to take CO2 directly out of the air. It is also proposed to take CO2 directly out of seawater. Several variations (liquid or solid absorbents) have been proposed and more will certainly come. The energy conditions for the entire DAC chain must, however, be assessed more thoroughly. DAC requires energy that also causes emissions if one relates to the current energy system. The starting point for doing ppm separation at atmospheric pressure and high-pressure injection into reservoirs is very unfavourable. The gain can quickly turn into a loss.

The proposals put forward are presented in the media with broad perspectives as "the solution". "Look here, this is how it can be done!" Demo facilities are being built to show how close this is to realisation. "see it works!"; or does it really? After all, this must work in the big perspective if it is to have any value. The connection to the Last-power is an obvious perspective. Wikipedia refers {27} to a publication [19], that claims that regardless of which fossil energy source is used, DAC will result in greater CO_2 emissions than what is captured. And as we know: Regardless of which electricity is used, in phase 1, it will have an effect that results in the same CO_2 emissions as coal power.

According to the IEA, a representative estimate for energy consumption for direct air capture is around 0.22 oil equivalents/ton CO_2 captured. With the facts that the oil has a density of 800 kg/m^3 and that 85% of this is carbon, burning this oil equivalently gives approx. 1.8 tons of CO_2. If efficiency is also taken into account, for example, in the heating and production of this amount of energy, the CO_2 emissions will be significantly higher. Most of the energy use is in the form of heat, which makes it possible to reduce the required power supply. Perhaps, it is not entirely coincidental that the "demo-DAC" is made in Iceland.

So far, it's hard to take this seriously. What was established by the demo-DAC stands today and causes higher CO_2 emissions. The symbolism is extremely powerful, but it seems clear that DAC is part of the problem and not part of the solution. This is most similar to creative business activity.

5.3. Illusory and Real Power

5.3.1. Earmarking

Technically speaking, it is the Last-power that determines the real carbon footprint, i.e., the CO_2 emission. Physics and logic say it is! We have explained this thoroughly and elaborately because in the media we hear very little about this side of the matter. But in the "business world", another phenomenon appears: earmarking of power, "annexation" of low-emission power.

A better power quality than what is professionally, physically and technically correct, or even possible, is bought out of the system. When working at the ACER and macro level, as we do, it does not matter who uses electricity for what and where. It is the case that no matter who increases the total electricity use, it is the Last-power that increases. In a macro scale, all other power is used to the maximum, only the Last-power can increase. So even if you have bought low-emission electricity, the total electricity consumption goes up and "your" electricity causes the Last-power to increase. Simple and irrefutable logic.

Earmarked power is a classic example of an illusion that exists in good health. You can disregard the physical system by buying a piece of paper on freedom from emissions. If someone one day buys, e.g., all the renewable energy in Finland to use on oil platforms in Norway, then suddenly there is no renewable energy left in Finland, or…? Is this metaphysics or economics? It is very un-technical and un-physical. We are really in "indulgence" now.

You know Luther in the 16th century wanted away from a church that largely used indulgences. One is willing to pay to obtain an advantage. Substance or not. As long as the illusion lives, this has immeasurably great economic/political value, for some.

5.3.2. The residual energy mix and carbon footprint

5.3.2.1. Power properties for sale

This book is very much about the fact that it is the Last-power that determines the carbon footprint in a professional context. But, at the same time, the residual power mix is a "local" real aspect that can be mentioned. Norwegian Water Resources and Energy Directorate (NVE) keeps track of it, but we hear little about it in the media. The residual power mixture is very unpopular, it is best not to talk about it.

It's amazing what can be sold. Creative economy lies in time and the product can be almost anything as long as it is perceived to have value. 'I've bought a lot of weird stuff over the years,' says Roy.

The "residual power mix" in Norway is a small curiosity in that context. It is important to understand the consequences of electrification in Norway and whether geography plays a role, or not.

In English, the residual power mixture is called the "European residual mixture". The strange thing is that Norway sells out most of its renewable hydro energy, and has done so for many years already.

Who would have thought that? Or the correct thing to say is that we sell out the pure properties of renewable hydro energy. We do not sell the power itself but the "properties", which means a low carbon footprint. That is why the "residual power mixture" is also called the "national product declaration" given by NVE. Everyone who sells "goods" is required to label the contents these days. It means that someone pays to exchange dirty power for clean power. As long as there is enough physical power on both sides of the trade, this can be done with a couple of mouse clicks. Even the cable connection to Europe is completely unimportant in that context.

It's a pure barter where the power industry gets paid well for just having given someone a better conscience and reputation and without anyone getting a worse conscience and reputation. Another example of money being thicker than CO_2. ACER works so that everyone in Europe has equal access to renewable energy, regardless of geography. It, therefore, does not really matter where it is produced. There is (or at least it was) apparently something called the renewables directive from Brussels that governs the guarantees of origin.

Selling guarantees of origin outside the country reduces the quality of the power here at home. What we get in exchange is bad stuff. Thus, we are left here with a high carbon footprint. In recent years, approximately 100 TWh of the approximately 120 TWh we produce have been sold. But can't we sell out the pure qualities of our power and at the same time continue to claim that we have pure power? No, we can't because power can't be used twice. This means that most of the clean Norwegian hydropower is very dirty. Despite this, "clean Norwegian hydropower" is a fundamental premise for Norwegian climate policy. This cannot be characterised as anything other than a gross lie, or should we call it fraud?

The carbon footprint for the Norwegian residual power mix has been quite high in recent years, at the level of gas power. In 2016–2017, the residual power was somewhere between 520–540 g/kWh. For comparison, coal power has a carbon footprint in the range of 800–1200 g/kWh and gas power approximately 500 g/kWh.

5.3.2.2. The primary cause of carbon footprint

The following paragraph presents some impact statements based on Norway's residual power. The real consequences will be based on the Last-power's carbon footprint. However, the examples based on residual power nevertheless illustrate how terribly wrong it is in Norway to assume that electricity has zero carbon footprint. Regardless of what one thinks about the Last-power, everyone must have understood that the residual power is the cleanest power you can count on. That those behind, e.g., Climate cure30, NVE and Statkraft (Environment Directorate, Norwegian Road Administration, Coastal Administration, Directorate of Agriculture, Norwegian Water Resources and Energy Directorate and ENOVA) do not take this into account is very revealing.

They play a high game. Within these organisations, there must be many professionals who understand the realities surrounding this. How they got all these not to protest is a very interesting question.

For an estimate of the carbon footprint of electrified transport, it is necessary to start with the different carbon intensities for different types of power generation. The figures below are taken from NVE's website a couple of years ago. It is easy to see that coal power is by far the most CO_2-intensive power. That is why we say that the focus must be on removing coal power, today's Last-power, before we electrify, because it is dramatically much worse than the others.

Coal power	1119 g CO_2/kWh
Gas power	514 g CO_2/kWh
Wind power	14 g CO_2/kWh
Nuclear power	13 g CO_2/kWh (0.81 mg radioactive waste/kWh)
Hydropower	17 g CO_2/kWh

In the residual power in Norway, it is stated that a large proportion of "fossil power" is included. If one assumes that it consists of the same relative ratio between coal and gas as in Germany, one arrives roughly at the figure stated below. If there is more coal, the carbon intensity will be significantly higher.

The CO_2 intensity of Norwegian residual power: approx. 530 g CO_2/kWh

- The pool (entire EU): approx. 300 g CO_2/kWh

5.3.2.3. Emissions from direct electrified transport

We can exemplify emissions with a small and a large electric car of the usual kind. We must take into account that consumption varies from a low level in ideal conditions to higher levels due to different conditions, drivers, driving patterns, tyre pressure, temperature, wind, altitude, etc. The most representative electricity consumption for movement is perhaps around the middle of the values which we state further below. As you know, mileage is significantly reduced on cold days. The batteries have to be charged more often on cold days. This also reduces the winter time energy efficiency.

An article in Solar Reviews: "…cold weather makes the batteries work harder, and drains more power in the process…" It is also important to put the figures that emerge into the purported "zero emissions perspective" that is promoted so strongly. By multiplying consumption by intensity, you then get an estimate of how big the emissions are, as shown below.

BMW i3 (consumption):	*0.15–0.25 kWh/km (approx. 1400 kg net weight)*
Intensity (residual power):	79–132 g CO2/km
Intensity (coal power):	168–280 g CO2/km
Tesla X (consumption):	*0.20–0.31 kWh/km (approx. 2400 kg net weight)*
Intensity (residual power):	105–163 g CO2/km
Intensity (coal power):	224–347 g CO2/km

No zero emissions here! These CO2 emissions must be compared with the emissions of ordinary fossil-fuel cars. Some typical values are given below for cars of slightly different sizes. Here, driving patterns and many other factors come into play but the figures are representative. 'Like I said, I'm buying an electric car anyway,' says Roy.

Medium segment (2018):	118 g CO2/km
SUV (2018):	132 g CO2/km
New small cars:	104 g CO2/km

Anyway, it is not an unreasonable claim that a coal-powered electric car emits about twice as much CO2 as a normal car. And, of course, only to the operation of the car! Operation is what is assessed in these figures. The production of the battery is a matter that also increases power consumption. We will hear more about that when it becomes clear how much power the battery factories planned in Norway will require. There are also many other losses that are not mentioned, such as power transmission, charge loss, heating of the passenger compartment, and self-discharge of the batteries. It comes on top.

This agrees well with what is estimated with the Formula no. [5b] in Chapter 2.2.3. An electric car emits approx. twice as much CO2 as an equally heavy fossil car!

5.3.2.4. Emissions from e-hydrogen

Green hydrogen as a fuel is another current issue when it comes to transport. For example, a Hyundai Nexo hydrogen car (approx. 1850 kg net weight) tested over time is reported to use approx. 0.011 kg H2/km. As 1 kg of H2 corresponds to 33.3 kWh of energy, this means an average consumption of 0.37 kWh/km. But since the energy efficiency of the production of hydrogen is about 30%, the global CO2 emission from hydrogen power will be approx. 3 times larger than coal power if all the "wasted" energy comes from power (See Chapter 3.6).

This surely is valid for "green hydrogen", produced by electrolysis, and for "blue hydrogen", produced from natural gas, the factor 3 perhaps should be reduced because power to some extent may be replaced by heat which otherwise would have been wasted.

- Intensity (residual power): approx. 0.6 kg CO2/km (= 3 * 0.37 * 0.53 g CO2/kWh)
- Intensity (coal power): approx. 1.2 kg CO2/km (= 3 * 0.37 * 1.11 kg CO2/kWh)

Yes, these are high numbers, striking and significantly higher than the emissions from direct electrification because the production of hydrogen and especially liquid e-fuels is very energy-intensive. For liquid e-fuels (Chapter 3.7.1), we must multiply the CO2 intensity by another factor of 3 compared to hydrogen. Then we reach the range of 3.6 kg CO2/km and higher. A completely different league from both directly electrified and fossil. But it is claimed by some (and is uncontested by all) that hydrogen is the solution. Truly incredible, but it joins the incredible array of "solutions".

Summary Chapter 5

- Both Norwegian and EU's reduction plans are obviously unrealistic and only politically and not thoroughly scientifically based.

- The big problem for any changeover is the enormous dependence on fossil power. Globally, fossil fuels make up a whopping 86%, of which coal is 30%.
- The Norwegian reduction plans will increase emissions outside Norwegian borders.
- Germany is increasing renewables strongly and has far too little Infill-power. It puts the system under pressure (Power loss likely).
- CCS was going to save the world! Great expectations, which cannot be fulfilled! "Build facilities" but lack ready-to-build technological solutions. Today's technologies, which are still immature, are inefficient and will require far too many resources if they are to be developed so that CCS will mean something for the climate. (But as shown earlier: By use of the oxyfuel technique CCS is significantly improved and may be acceptable.)
- CCS requires a lot of energy. To use it on high CO_2 concentrations would be the least ineffective, but most sources are very lean Moderate estimate: 1 kWh/kg CO_2, the same as emissions from coal power, means net-zero CO_2 reduction in the atmosphere.
- For the capture of European emissions, 2,500 Mtons CO_2, 2,500 TWh of energy is required, or more.
- CCS can perhaps capture 60–80% of exhaust gas from large sources. It is highly unclear how much net CO_2 is stored in relation to how large CO_2 emissions it causes. In any case, CCS has no place while the Last-power is coal power.
- Still uncertain about efficiency (the energy balances and the consequences that follow are not discussed/stated!).
- An extremely large number of facilities are required for CCS to have any real impact on the climate.
- CCS can be used in oil production for CO_2 reinjection and pressure support ("business case"). Whether it has any purpose for the climate is unlikely.
- Amines are used as liquid absorbents in CCS. Amines are highly questionable both for the environment and the climate.
- Safety in the event of leaks must be ensured (air, water).
- Energy consumption in CCS is very high. Economics overrides physical and chemical facts.

- Low CO2 concentrations => low efficiency and high energy consumption. It is no coincidence that the "demo-DAC" was made in Iceland where there are lot of "free heat" in nature.
- Earmarking of "zero emission power"—an illusion/indulgence for a better conscience. And many people need that. Otherwise no effect.
- The residual power mix has a somewhat higher carbon footprint than gas power.
- The properties of hydropower are sold via guarantees of origin, but no real climate effects are included. A disgusting game for the gallery! Residual power: approx. 530 g CO2/kWh.
- Practical examples for some cars with Last-power and residual power and an example from e-hydrogen.

6. Nuclear Power

6.1. The Need for Nuclear Power

While working with this thematic for 5-6 years, we have become increasingly convinced that the world is going in the wrong direction regarding climate concerns. As described in the previous chapters, it is obvious that the two major tools in the fight against CO_2 are based on 1) electrification and 2) renewable power in the form of unstable wind and sun power. As we have shown previously in this book, most electrifications significantly increase CO_2 emissions as long as coal power is the Last-power. Now we will show that wind and sun power are not the right tools for increasing the most important tool for fighting the climate crisis: Electricity!

Ooooops! Did we not just right the opposite: Electrifications increase CO_2 emissions? Yes, we did; we were right—the effect of electrification depends on the crucial timing of "when we do what"! The climate's worst enemy is coal power and as we have shown: As long as coal power is the Last-power, the only effective means is to reduce the coal power, so the quicker we get rid of it, the better for the climate => We must produce as much low-emission electricity as possible as fast as possible and use it for replacing the coal power! Easy to understand, easy to do.

But both the production and distribution of electricity are complicated; they are based on the laws and consequences of the thermodynamic laws. One of the consequences is that it is not easy to store electric power as such. Yes, we do have batteries but in the enormous amounts of energy we are talking about now, batteries can't be used. Yes, we also have other ways to store electric energy: We can transform the electric energy to another form of energy like pump power as described in Chapter 3.4.1. But in practice, that is very difficult to achieve for so enormous amounts of energy. And we can store electrical energy in the form of chemical energy, like hydrogen.

But as we have written in Chapter 3.6, since the process, Electric energy -> hydrogen -> electric energy has an energy efficiency as low as 30%, we waste 70% of the energy we produce. In the situation we are now, we can't afford that. (Possibly this may be significantly improved by the use of the oxyfuel method, Chapter 3.7.5.)

But wind and sun power are unstable, sometimes they produce too much, sometimes too little, and we don't have sufficient good means to store the surplus energy when we produce too much => We need an extra electricity source which we can regulate such that we always have as much electricity as we need. Today, we solve this problem by interaction between wind and sun-power and some other energy source which is easily regulated, the so-called Infill-power which must have good dynamic properties, in practice, it turns out to be either gas or coal power.

But the electric system must always have enough energy input—just as much as the output, the current need, if not it collapses. And we have no control over the need, power is switched on and off all the time. The good thing, however, is that since there are so many damned switches, the sum of the need normally does not change very fast so the system manages to keep up. (And personally, we are very impressed that the system manages even major accidents like break of power lines, etc. And we don't have the faintest idea of how they do that.)

Anyway, it normally works well.

But that is because we have enough input power. Ideally, this should be Infill-power that has the ability to store the surplus energy from wind and sun-power, but in practice, most of this energy is taken from the existing electric net, which in practice means the Last-power, coal power, or if we are lucky, gas power. This is an accident of limited scope, it depends on how often and to which extent this happens. But the volume of the Infill-power has to be at least as large as the total sum of wind and sun power for the actual area, if not the electric net will break down. Germany has had a few narrow escapes in that respect.

But if we look into the promised land in some future when we are well into phase 3, what will the situation be then? If all of the normal electricity needs are covered by wind and sun-power, this means that we need just as much Infill-power as the maximum volume of wind and sun power.

So the needed or necessary total electric available power will equal: [9]Available stable power + 2 * total wind and sun-power.

So the more wind and sun power there is in the actual region, the more actually redundant Infill-power is needed. It is clear without saying that also the electric net has to cover this unnecessary extra flow of electricity, somewhat depending on the locations of power production and consumer sites.

To be honest, this is not the whole truth. There are circumstances that make equation [9] a little less true:

In a situation where pumping power can be built relatively cheaply and easily, such as, e.g., in Norway, Infill-power can be obtained relatively easily in terms of the amount of kWh. But the problem with the effect still remains because pumping power does not increase the effect; to do that, you also have to get more generators. How big this problem is depends on factors such as what is the maximum power needed in relation to the amount of power available when wind and solar power do not supply anything. Geography also comes into the concept.

However, we ignore this question in the rest of this book.

The minimum total power needed according to [9] is when total wind and sun power equals zero. If we could plan the future net from the beginning, let's say a few decades ago, we would of course replace the wind and sun-power with stable flexible low-emission power: 4th-Generation Nuclear Power, 4GNP. So now we have to pay for our lack of insight and technical abilities a few decades ago and apparently, until today. But tomorrow? Now we know that we are very close to the situation when this problem may be solved by 4GNP!

6.2. Types of Nuclear Power

There are many types of nuclear power.

6.2.1. Fusion nuclear power

This is the final goal: If we can succeed in producing power by fusion nuclear {28} power in a safe8and reliable way, we can forget about any other way to produce power. In recent years, there has been a significant improvement in research into this, which has been going on since the 50s. But we still may be decades from being able to produce working fusion nuclear power plants, and there is of course the possibility that we never will be able to achieve this goal. From a practical point of view: Forget any practical help from fusion nuclear energy until we have it.

But don't forget to continue, even intensify the research on fusion nuclear power! Because this technology has infinite access to fuel, which is water, even though the water needs some advanced processing before it can be used. And perhaps even better: In practice, there is no waste problem.

So of course: Research must go on!

6.2.2. 2nd and 3rd generation fission nuclear power

This is where we are today. But do we want to stay here? No, we don't; we must progress and improve. Perhaps primarily due to the waste and fuel problem. They seemingly are manageable, but expensive and cumbersome and perhaps the worst: They have a bad reputation. Although today's nuclear power is very safe, we should proceed to the 4th generation of fission power which has many good properties worth waiting for.

6.2.3. 4th-generation nuclear power, 4GNP

This is the close future and as for today, what we have to go for: The salvation of our world is based on this for the first coming decades. This article {29} gives a good overview of 4GNP {30} reactors.

In Sweden, they have worked with 4GNP for some time. Another rather thorough description of one of the 4GNP types: Molten Salt Reactors. {31}

Within 4GNP, we can sort by size based on power production in MW. For the sake of simplicity, we here only distinguish between small modular reactors, SMR, less than 300 MW, and large reactors. To put the size in perspective:

- The largest 2nd and 3rd generation nuclear power stations range from 8212 MW in China to the 10th largest of 4748 MW in South Korea.
- The largest hydropower station is also in China and has a capacity of 22.500 MW. There are 7 hydropower stations in the world which have a capacity of 10.000 MW or more.

Small modular reactors, {32} SMR gives a relatively detailed and thorough description of the most important types of SMRs. IEAEs Advances in Small Modular Reactor Technology {33} Developments gives even rather detailed information, including a list of all SMRs in the world pr. 2022.

One of the main advantages of small reactors is their limited size which makes mass production possible. SMRs will also be very flexible when it comes to installation in an existing electric net.

This will save a lot of money and other resources because of lessening the need for net/grid adaptions.

We are on the doorstep of this technology: Today, there are more than 80 projects at one stage or another project. The project that has come the farthest is probably the Chinese project 210 MW {34} which has delivered power to the electric net for about 2 years. The Chinese 2 MW {35} is also an interesting project.

Safety:

We now have enough nuclear power in the world for the statistics to give good answers on safety. Today, there are more than 450 active nuclear power plants in the world. But statistically, nuclear power is the safest form of electricity: No other type of power has fewer deaths per produced number of kWh. Steven Pinker, Professor of Psychology, Harvard University, and author of books in his book *Enlightenment Now* (2021) gives the number of deaths pr. kWh relative to nuclear power:

Source of power:

Number of deaths rel. nuclear power	
Natural gas	38
Biomass	63
Petroleum products	243
Coal	387

Obviously, the security of nuclear power obviously is far better than its reputation. The SMRs also have inbuilt safety in that the reactor automatically shuts down in a critical situation.

Nuclear power has a bad reputation due to a couple of major accidents. The irrational fear of nuclear power is and has been the biggest obstacle to implementing nuclear power in many countries. Our belief is that the intensive development of nuclear power can only be stopped by illusions that few politicians dare to challenge.

But now, the EU has decided that nuclear power is green, hopefully, that will shortly kill a lot of illusions. France is a big supporter of nuclear power with its approx. 50 plants, while Germany has decided to wind them down. We are anxiously awaiting what happens in this matter, but have good hope that nuclear power will eventually be accepted as a safe, cheap, and efficient low-emission energy source and the only one which may enable us to come close to the climate targets.

Fuel:

The 4GNP plants can use both thorium and waste from generation 2 and 3 reactors as fuel. Thorium is not radioactive and must therefore be used together with enriched uranium. The advantage is that there is far more thorium than uranium in nature and that the waste problems are far less than for generation 2 and 3 reactors. (This is particularly interesting for Norway since there are large quantities of thorium in Norway. Again, Norway is unbelievably lucky with raw resources.)

Reusing waste uranium and leaving a waste which has far less radiation and with a much shorter half-life time, also reduces the waste problem significantly.

Economy:

Today, it is very difficult to judge the final economy of SMRs, we just do not have the needed experience. However, the possibility for mass production, the large availability of relatively cheap fuel, and the relatively easy waste handling give good reason to expect a significant reduction in the price of nuclear power. A very important question is, however: Will SMRs last as long as today's nuclear reactors?

But due to the unstable wind and sun power which need about as much Infill-power as the power they may produce themselves, it is overwhelming probably that SMRs, and also power from larger 4th generation reactors' time, will be much cheaper over a lifetime.

Application potential:

SMRs can be produced small enough to be used for operating ships, probably also for relatively small ships. We have already used generation 2 nuclear power for the drift of submarines. With the possibility of mass production of 4GNP, this is the obvious solution for ships. The only limitation of the use of 4GNP is the human imagination. Application potential is large, with wide flexibility in scale.

Time perspective:

Since there already are more than 80 4GNP projects around the world, of which a few already have delivered power to the electric net for some years, it is obvious that it is possible to start mass production of 4GNP in 5–10 years. Some bottlenecks will appear that should be handled as soon as possible. When we are able to mass produce 4GNP, there are no limits for the use of it. No other low-emission power can compete with this. The only rational way to handle the climate crises is to put all available resources into mass production of 4GNP ASAP; not to mention how happy birds and nature will be to get rid of wind power.

In fact, the best thing for the climate would be not to start any new wind and solar power projects. We already have too many of them.

6.3 A Plan for Implementation of 4GNP

Until now, the development of low-emission power has mainly been through wind/solar power. That development must be replaced by sufficient development of 4GNP, such that we as soon as possible will be able to mass produce 4GNP. This should be done by global planning and cooperation. When we are waiting for the 4GNPs, we should stop all new wind and sun-power plans. For already started projects, the following points should be considered:

1) We must have as much Infill-power as the sum of wind and solar power.
2) All development of wind and solar power must be followed by an equal development of Infill-power. That is why wind and solar power should be kept at a minimum.
3) Hydropower plants must have reservoirs large enough not to run empty, or they must be pump power stations.
4) Pumping power stations should be prioritised because they can store the surplus energy from wind and solar power. The energy efficiency of these normally is about 80%.

5) Total power should be equal to the sum of stable low-emission power and twice that of wind and solar power.
6) In all cases, it should be considered for which area the plans are valid and what are the consequences for the electric net.

Considering the scope, scarcity and premise of "power without carbon", it is obvious that we must develop 4GNP! Why wait when it can reduce the disturbance in nature and the instability that comes with wind/solar power? It is probably possible to mass produce 4GNP in the late 2020s or early 2030s. There are already many working prototypes.

The alternative is:

1) Continued development of wind and sun power
2) Development of sufficient low-emission Infill-power and
3) Along with the heavy strengthening of the electric net.

A lot of R&D and other skill-building is required before mass production of 4GNP. The closed classic nuclear power plants that are still functional can contribute carbon-free.

Energy saving is effective because it is the marginal-power of coal power that is reduced. First of all, all unnecessary electrifications must be delayed/stopped and coal power phased out.

That everything should be electrified "now" and that it is good for the climate is therefore a big lie. Development of inefficient technologies such as producing hydrogen must be stopped immediately. These are dead ends in phases 1 and 2, i.e., for many decades. When we come to phase 3, we don't need hydrogen any more. In the future, we must be secure and live with the supply of safe and stable power, not from the development of unstable power along with as much redundant low-emission power.

Summary Chapter 6

- The necessary total sum of power equals

- Available stable power + 2 * total wind and sun power.

- To avoid the production of redundant energy, we should stop the development of wind and sun power. Instead, we should put all available resources into the production of 4GNP. It is very likely that mass production of 4GNP will be possible within 5–10 years.
- Research on fusion nuclear power should go on.
- So far nuclear power (1st to 3rd generation reactors) has been the safest energy source. 4GNP reactors will be even safer.
- We can't give good estimates of the economy of 4GNP today, but it's overwhelmingly probable that 4GNP power will be far cheaper than wind and sun power.

7. Weaknesses of CO2 Taxes And Climate Quotas

7.1. National CO2 Taxes

National CO2 taxes {36} have existed since 1990. The table of National CO2 taxes shows that there is a big difference both in terms of tax level and what is covered by the allowances. These fees will also apply to areas that are not covered by the climate quotas. Nations themselves can choose the level of both the scope of what they want to tax and the size of the tax itself measured in price per ton of emitted CO2.

It may look as if this uses a good market principle: Put a high price on what you don't want. And if things had worked as politicians both in Norway and the EU Commission believe, then this would have been fine. But Ibsen understood much of how this can work: "When the starting point is the wrongest, the result is the strangest". So here the effect will be that you electrify like crazy. Surely that must reduce the emissions?

"But those of you who have read this far in this book understand why this works against its purpose: When the Last-power is coal power, the production of the extra electricity needed for electrification will usually result in much greater global CO2 emissions than the same process emitted with fossil energy. And the increased electricity consumption will make it even more difficult to phase out coal power. This is a tax that works against its purpose, at least in countries like Norway. But since we are so magnificent, we are still among those with the highest tax. That's how we're the best!"

And it gets even worse: the EU Commission has also decided that each individual nation's physical CO2 emissions must be counted. And that's luck for Norway: All the CO2 emissions we save by electrifying, e.g., the oil platforms' approx. 15–25 TWh, are charged to the coal power producers in Europe and to the atmosphere.

7.2. CO2 Border Taxes

The EU Commission has proposed a new CO2 tax that will apply from 2026: CO2 border tax. {37}. The purpose of this tax is to protect European industry against imports from competitors who do not have CO2 taxes or climate quota requirements linked to their production of CO2-intensive products: Carbon-intensive steel, aluminium, cement, fertiliser, and electricity. This is interesting because the production of these substances is considered CO2 intensive, and electrical power is the common denominator for all these products. Imagine that! This is something Norwegian politicians must note: Electric power has a CO2 footprint!

In practice, the scheme will start and function as follows:

Those who import must pay a carbon tax (Carbon Border Adjustment Mechanism, CBAM) which corresponds to what they would have to pay if the goods were produced in the EU with the EU's rules for carbon pricing.

If a producer from a non-EU country can prove that they have already paid the carbon tax, it will be deducted from CBAM.

The entire scheme is to be phased in gradually until 2036.

7.3. Climate Quotas

7.3.1. But surely the climate quotas solve all the problems?

The most common argument that we face against our message is, "It does not matter, the quotas will solve it efficiently", meaning this is not a matter to be discussed. Quotas work very well as a domination technique. But let's take a closer look at this aspect.

We have now explained how it all fits together, how the system dynamics work and what we must do and when (the phases) so that we have a realistic plan to reduce/solve our climate problems. We believe that what the plan lacks in enthusiasm and optimism, it makes up for in realism and efficiency. We have shown that the EU's plan for reducing CO2 emissions has built-in mechanisms that lead to many difficult and expensive measures leading to significantly increased emissions when they are implemented at the wrong time and with premises that do not match reality.

It is bad for both the climate and the economy; we waste a lot of capital on measures that work against their purpose. Less money will be left for measures that actually will work when the time is right.

In fact, the belief that the climate quotas will work leads to a reduced effort for measures that really reduce CO2 emissions.

Many, and especially social economists and others who have no idea about physics and chemistry, are assuring society with high confidence that the problems are solved by the climate quotas.

When it becomes too expensive to emit CO2, well, you don't do it. Is that so? Maybe we need to look a little closer to this.

If quota prices become too high, the power prices will be very high and the "comfortable life" of EU citizens will be threatened. But politicians want re-election both for themselves and their party.

There are, therefore, limits to what politicians will take responsibility for. They will not dare to adopt regulations that lead to a major shortage of electric power.

A realistic assessment shows that electricity demand will increase dramatically much more than the increase in low-emission power. Result: All of the available electrical power will be used, also including coal power.

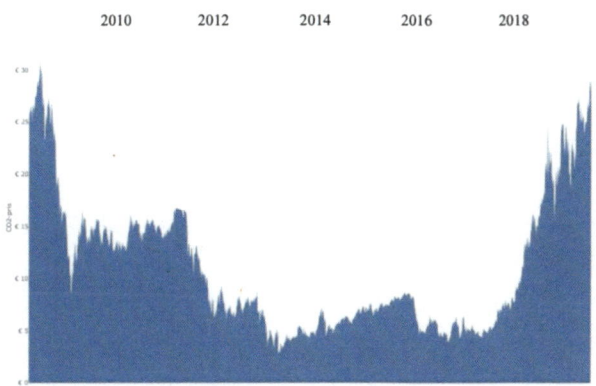

Figure 7.1: Digital channel for the energy industry {38} [enerWE]: The quota price in the EU from 2008 to October 2019. Price range for the amplitudes in this diagram is from € 0–30

In practice, the quotas are useless as a tool for reducing CO_2 emissions when there is too little electricity to maintain a normal life in the EU. In other words, the quotas will not work when needed and the coal power production will go on.

Today, such an enormous increase in electricity consumption is planned that it is not physically possible to meet the increased electricity consumption without the consumption of coal power also increasing. And then, "Our Formula" applies with coal power as the Last-power. The CO_2 emissions for many/most processes will roughly double. It will vary slightly from process to process how large the increase in CO_2 emissions will be. This cannot be debated away from. That's how it is.

And even worse: If the Last-power (against presumption) should be/become gas power, while coal power is still needed to meet the energy demand, the total emission of CO_2 will be even greater, even though it is gas power that increases and decreases in line with consumption. This is because coal power will then increase at the expense of gas power as long as there are available coal power plants. Because in a market-driven system, it will always be the case that money is thicker than CO_2. This was the case in the period between 2012 and 2018 when quota prices were very low. See Figure 7.1.

At that time, coal power production was high and gas power production was so low that many gas power plants were unproductive. But around 2018/2019, climate quota prices increased so much that coal power became the Last-power and coal power production fell. In this sense, this worked according to theory.

The quota prizes increased very much until they stabilised at the beginning of the 20s, then fell from the end of 2023 (Fig 7.2). Note the amplitude range difference in **Figure 7.1** and **Figure 7.2**

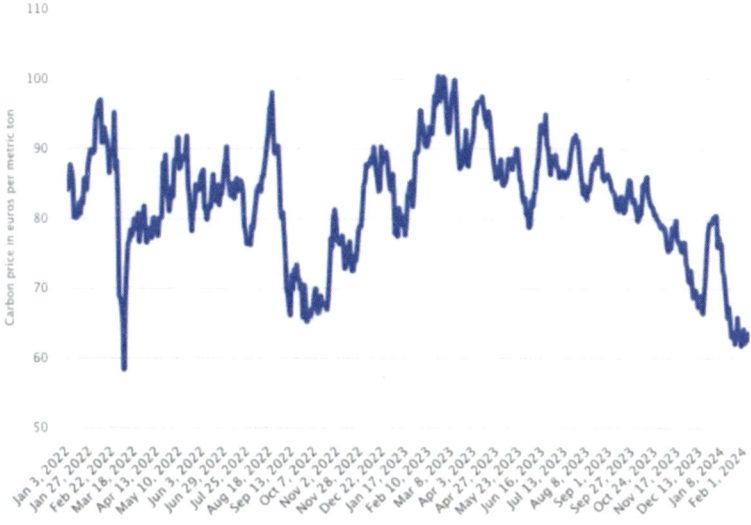

Figure 7.2: EU quota prizes {39} from January 2022 to February 2024. Statista. Price range for the amplitudes in this diagram is from € 50–110.

It is important that the reason for the reduction of coal power from 2018 to 2020 is understood, otherwise, the statistics on coal-fired power production will be misused as a kind of proof that electrification does not lead to increased coal-fired power. The decline in coal-fired power generation will not continue when all the gas power reserves have been put into use. Then the unreasonable electrification will cause coal power production to increase again. Then it doesn't help that coal power is kept expensive due to high quota prices; the world *must* have electricity, and climate quotas can't do magic.

They can't provide enough Infill-power and nuclear power and they can't build pump power plants that are necessary to prevent the power system from collapsing.

But what we can do is intensify the development of 4th generation nuclear power, but that is treated in Chapter 6.

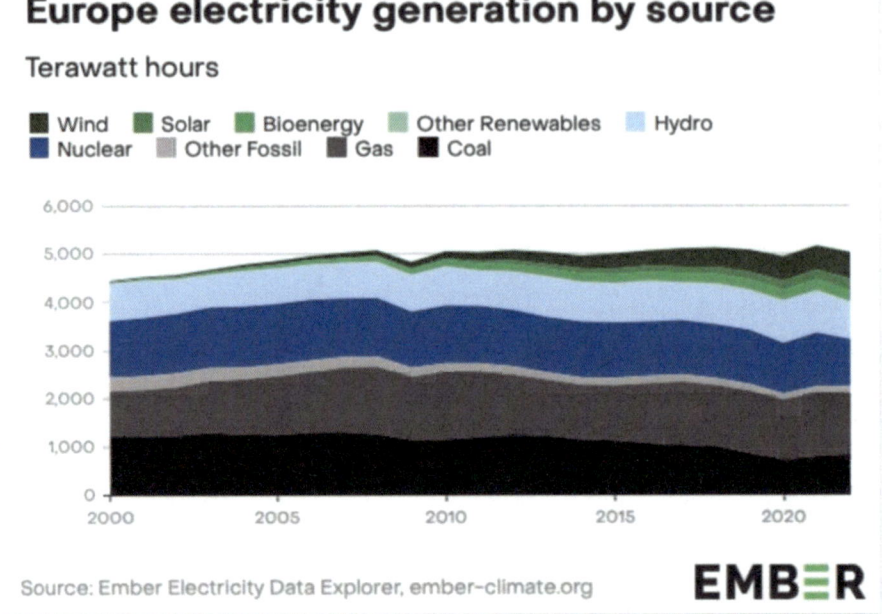

Figure 7.3: Europe electricity generation by source.

Figure 7.4 gives a clear indication that climate quotas do not work. Note the difference between plans and reality.

When the lack of electricity causes prices to multiply, you do not get electricity to keep an apartment, let alone a house, warm, even charging a mobile phone becomes expensive and…

Of course, that doesn't happen because the politicians quickly understand that such conditions create political upheaval and they have no other choice: Increase the amount of climate quotas and let the coal power plants loose; WE MUST HAVE ELECTRICITY!

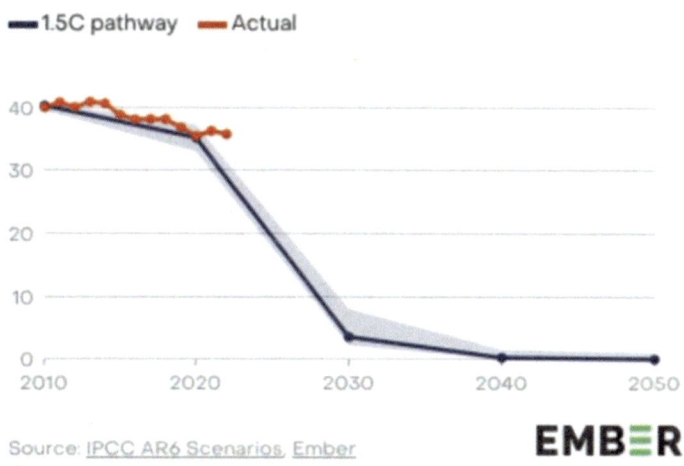

Figure 7.4: The share of coal in the mix needed for a sustainable 1.5C pathway.

7.3.2. Have we become too many?

It is no coincidence that we have not written anything about what is perhaps the biggest problem. It is a difficult matter, which cannot be resolved; at least not by us. The only thing we achieve by raising that issue is that even more people will stigmatise us. 'This must be about Earth's population,' says Roy.

Because the earth's population is continuously increasing and has been doing so for far too long and far too much, it is perhaps the most direct cause of the atmosphere's increasing CO2 content.

So why not stop population growth? With fewer people on earth, the better off everyone will be. And everyone must think that's nice, right?

But then there is this thing about genes. Man as a relatively intelligent being has existed for about 40,000 years, and the basis for many of our genes is much older than that. The question of the earth's overpopulation has only become a topical issue, let's say, in the last 50 years. When Per was a boy, they learned at school that the earth's population was approx. 2 billion, today it is more than 7 billion. We cannot wait 40,000 years for the genes to be "modernised" before we solve this problem.

'We have to use the right head,' says Roy.

Summary Chapter 7

- "When the starting point is the wrongest, the result is the strangest." The effect of the climate taxes is that people want to electrify like crazy because that must reduce CO_2 emissions. No, unfortunately, Last-power applies!
- Norwegian electrification, such as the 15–25 TWh for offshore platforms, will in reality be charged to Europe, via the Last-power. Global CO_2 emissions will increase.
- The CO_2 quotas will have a limited effect when EU citizens' "comfortable life" is threatened. "Yellow vests" are something politicians fear.
- How big will the electricity crisis be when we have electrified oil platforms, transport and, in addition, CCS gobble up large amounts of energy? A plan for "consumption by nutrition" does not exist.
- Maybe there are too many of us on the planet! But what is certain is that there will be more of us.

8. Social Psychology

Our professional newspaper articles about the consequences of increased electrification in a still coal-fired world mostly triggered counter-articles where various techniques were used to protect and reinforce established illusions. We have, therefore, decided to take a closer look at the arena where opinions are influenced and perceptions are formed. There were prevailing illusions that stood in the way of a debate at a professional level.

8.1. What is an Illusion?

"Store Norske Leksikon" defines an illusion as: "Illusion is a sensory deception or a false perception that occurs spontaneously and is difficult to correct. In a figurative sense, it can mean unrealistic hope". They also include the illusion that is most common in our context: "Common misconceptions of connection (illusory correlations), causality (illusory control) and probabilities are often called cognitive illusions".

But the "Store Norske Lexicon" does not include the one that worries us the most: "Illusions that have been created for one purpose or another." Politics and advertising are full of such. In advertising, they probably know what they are doing, the politicians are perhaps more driven by idealism or pure and simple struggle for voters. Or, create a fundament for power and control.

Individuals are only small pieces in the system which, in the big picture, must rely on the great "collective" knowledge. In most areas, what we know ourselves is limited, and therefore we easily adopt "collective knowledge" as our own knowledge. But it turns out, again and again, that you can't trust "collective knowledge". Yes, it is claimed that one of the problems is that we are unable to distinguish between what we really know as individuals and what we know as a collective. The distinctions are blurred and we think we are more knowledgeable than we really are.

A little word of wisdom might be in order here:

Of your illusions, you only know those you have lost.

Frithjof Brandt, Danish philosopher.

8.2. We Don't Know What We Don't Know

"We don't know what we don't know"! Ignorance and knowledge are not two extremes. To not know is to be delusional!

Knowing what you don't know gives direction! Not wanting to know is a little constructive!

Not wanting to know what others know is in the category of stupidity!

Preventing the sharing of other people's knowledge is perhaps even worse, almost sabotage!

"We know what we don't know". If you talk to very enlightened and wise people about matters that they know a lot about, this sentence often hits your consciousness. We like to think: "This person knows an incredible amount about this, but most importantly, he knows what he doesn't know". That is the state we should strive for in every matter of importance: We must know what we don't know. It provides security for ourselves, and for those around us, and we understand what we have to do to move forward. It takes us in the right direction.

But precisely because we are aware that there is a lot we don't know, in this book we have chosen to place great demands on our claims. We have used mathematics, specialist knowledge, logic, secure data, and as factual a presentation as we could. And if we here and there are obviously unreasonable, yes, that is precisely the reason why we allow ourselves to be a little unreasonable.

During the work to promote our message, we have met many who do not want to know what we know. It has been a big and sad disappointment!

There is still much we do not know and we must look for new answers and connections.

8.3. A Bit About Illusions and What We Would Like to Believe

Humans have the characteristic that they easily accept to believe in something, perhaps it is even in our genes. For hundreds of thousands of years, decisions have been made based on feelings and beliefs, not on certain knowledge. (But preferably on the basis of logic based on faith and experience.) Humans have always believed, it is in our genes, but what they have believed in has changed throughout history.

As more and more knowledge was established, it slowly contributed to change. Influence from close surroundings was more important before, but now, in principle, the whole world could be influenced at the same time through the conscious use of various techniques through the media and the internet.

In our time, there are enormous opportunities for systematic influence and the whole world is at your disposal. Many see those opportunities, for better or for worse. It is going faster and faster, and a separate industry has emerged that knows exactly how to exploit it. The channels are ready for use. The temptation to take advantage of this is great. It's about power and control and it can be bought. Artificial intelligence (AI) has the potential to change the world completely and may both be a fantastic helper and a dangerous enemy.

A book by Anne Applebaum, *Democracy's Swan Song*, gives a frightening impression of what can await the democracies of today and the future. For some European democracies (Hungary, Poland, England, Italy), she describes larger and smaller groups that have tried to influence elections by deliberate lies, slander on the internet, etc. Anne Applebaum has both American and Polish citizenship and is a renowned author with, among other things, a Pulitzer Prize. She is married to Radosław Sikorski, who has been both defence and foreign minister in Poland.

The term influence society is not entirely far-fetched as a description of what we stand for. There is a razor-thin line between "true" and "false/illusory" information. Opinions must be influenced and managed. We write about that in this chapter.

8.3.1. How do illusions arise?

First of all, there must be something that is "sellable", something that goes straight to the core of our soul. The message must of course be accepted by many.

It may well be about life and death, the fear of the planet's demise, or just simply the possibility of obtaining advantages, such as easy money or many voters. Or, that it can give meaning to life for someone, such as the experience of justice; yes, it is often about "right and wrong" perceptions, pure ethics. It must be something that others can and will promote further so that the good news spreads.

A prerequisite for establishing illusions is that the message must be repeated many times. You need spreaders and spreading mechanisms. This seems like a pyramidal scheme combined with a contagious virus. It is a lot about ethics, the use of ethics, unfortunately sometimes also for dubious purposes.

There are large worldwide illusions and there are many small local ones that we live with on a daily basis, maybe without thinking much about it. We also have distinctive Norwegian illusions. That emission-free electricity is something of a matter which of course can be in that category. The illusions are there until one might, at some point, know better, but man is not particularly good at changing perceptions, especially not about what sits deep in the soul and is also experienced as beneficial. In some areas, it is possible to establish more and more knowledge, so that prevailing perceptions gradually change.

For example, many people who lived on our planet in historical times believed that the earth was flat. It was kind of provable because that's what it looks like from ground level with the naked eye. 'Flat as far as you can see! That's how it is in Nord-Trøndelag,' says Roy. Eventually, we gained certain knowledge that tells us that the earth is approximately round. Illusions can certainly also "disappear" if they are replaced by "something better", or another illusion.

Certain knowledge can kill illusions but it is a psychological fact that it takes a long time and requires good evidence and information channels to combat entrenched illusions, especially if they are also beneficial to many. Evolution over hundreds of thousands of years has put the will to believe into our genes. Take haunted houses, for example, especially in tourist spots. "We can't rule it out, can we?" applies in practice. Healing via special abilities like warm hands, etc. sells like never before. All the knowledge in the world will not be able to change this. If complicated knowledge is required to kill an illusion, of course, it is slow, or it is almost completely impossible.

A large proportion of the population is, after all, "illiterate" when it comes to expertise-heavy topics, such as energy systems. In sciences that are characterised by mathematical proofs to a lesser extent than the natural sciences, there is also a different culture for the debate. In sciences where nothing can be proven, there is much more room to discuss what constitutes facts. In these cultures, it is therefore easy to imagine that the respect for mathematical proofs is less than the respect people with a science background have for mathematical proofs.

8.3.2. How illusions control our thought processes

In today's society, social psychology and illusions are used to control our lives and influence our thoughts. These strategies are actively being used for example in politics and industry. Most people, therefore, cannot protect themselves from it either. Online newspapers and social media are extremely good spreaders in this context.

We must admit: We are afraid that "Artificial Intelligence" will be used by many for not very ethical purposes. And it is not simple to argue with a machine with unknown programs and information sources, not to speak of the programmer! This seems like a dangerous device for spreading and manipulating information. The "machines" can be provided with any objectives.

A lot is believed about a lot! Much is in the "will never be fact-checked" category. Many accept the belief to such an extent that it actually becomes a truth. It is a difficult balancing act if you are not particularly conscious. Everything is possible as long as the illusion is accepted.

Most people are more irrational than they care to know. We all face a limitation in relation to what we have good knowledge of, which we can claim to "know". What we do not know must necessarily be left to varying degrees of faith and uncertainty. Much of what we "know" may actually be "what we think we know". The boundary between faith and knowledge is probably quite fluid and relative. People have a hard time distinguishing between belief and knowledge,' says Roy.

It is terribly difficult for a physicist to believe in religion, it goes against most of the physical laws we know, and we know that miracles are impossible. 'Not in football,' says Roy. And it is very easy to understand that religion arose at a time when man could not explain any of the strange things that happened around them; yes, even the sun was a miracle! Yes, we can only recognise religion as an illusory phenomenon at this point.

There is still much we do not understand in this world, about our origins and many other things. It is one of the reasons why illusions can be easily created, we want to adopt the "knowledge". We know a lot today about how life can arise. Creating life has not yet succeeded, but we must remember that a billion years passed before the most primitive life started on earth. Doctoral candidates do not have quite that much time. This is primarily a matter of probabilities and coincidences. An extreme version of Darwin.

Another issue is who creates and what is the starting mechanism for illusions. History has shown time and time again that charismatic leaders can gather followers by starting illusions. Then it starts small and can become big. We know that the first thing that dies in a war is the truth. But it can also be done systematically, without charismatic leaders. Rich and global organisations such as The World Economic Forum (WEF) obviously have great opportunities to spread their message over most of the world. They admit, nay boast, that they now want to manipulate people into thinking the same as themselves.

In itself, this is not a new phenomenon—what are election campaigns—but now even "deliberate manipulation" seems to be allowed. The world moves on.

The internet and the media are the most important tools for social psychological manipulation; there is now really no limit to who can start the process. "Who" is in the background. It's just a matter of hitting a nerve at the right time. There are many who try all the time, and sometimes they succeed.

However, the main theme of this book is electrification and its consequences for CO_2 emissions, so let's get back to that.

8.4. On Electrification and Prevailing Illusions

Just so we are not misunderstood: Electrification will be an absolutely decisive factor in reducing CO_2 emissions, there is nothing wrong with electrification. The question is not "if" we should electrify but "when" to electrify, admittedly if certain decisive conditions are met. We have written a lot about that in this book.

It is not a question of whether there are illusions in the field of electrification. There are a lot of them and there is a lot of conscious illusion-building going on all the time. A word like greenwashing comes quite close. The supporters of electrification have figured out exactly how to market themselves. Electrification has been deliberately strongly linked to the climate issue and surfs well on that bubble. It has defined itself as climate technology, without reservation.

But when it comes to electrification, we have explained quite clearly elsewhere in the book that increased power demand in a system where low-emission powers are scarce, such as in Europe today, only leads to an increase in the use of coal power. And the consequence is that CO2 emissions increase. That is as far from zero emissions as you can get (see, e.g., Chap. 2). And, therefore, the CO2 accounts also do not measure up when it comes to documenting real emissions. We hope that this will be made crystal clear in this book. 'It doesn't add up to the facts,' says Roy.

But electrification has an obvious consequence: Increasing electricity prices! We see that very well these days (August 2022), even if what we see now is only an advanced power crisis due to some unfortunate coincidences: Failing gas supplies from Russia, failing winds in Europe and a very dry autumn, at least in southern Norway and large parts of Europe. But behind it all is electrification and it is only increasing. A natural question: Is this a deliberate development and by whom? We think the answer to the first part can be: Yes, many people make good money from this; both electricity and car manufacturers seem to get a good market from the prevailing climate policy.

But the good question is: Do these have enough influence to promote and preserve these illusions? They have many methods at their disposal, from lobbyists to commissioned research.

In the real, professional world, increased power consumption is far from "zero emissions", but it works surprisingly well as a "shell hide". The real emissions in an overall perspective are camouflaged and hidden away or made harmless. It is almost a little comical that a small insignificant word can have such a strong influence. We must, therefore, delve deeply into social psychology to understand why it is so difficult to come up with facts about the consequences of electrification, and why hard facts and comprehensive thinking do not gain wider acceptance. There is a lack of channels to get the message across.

After all, we have experienced that many in the "establishment" assume the role of defenders of the "correct" view. In the media, we have encountered debate editors who stop an article, obviously because of their conviction that we are wrong. These are probably just the executive arm of the newsroom.

It can also be mentioned that researchers and some professors have also placed themselves on the "correct" branch. They are very eager to shoot down anything that does not fit into the business plan, mostly using dominating techniques and, to a lesser extent, persuasive knowledge and logic.

Only what fits the main purpose should be communicated. They are not impressed by energy balances and thermodynamics, but they should be part of the subject. When you read what the professors we have debated with write, it is to be understood that they are so wise and know so much that we have to trust them. It is an indulgence that this is too complicated for "little us" to understand properly. Academic integrity is no longer a matter of course.

Some gain benefits or wish to continue these benefits by promoting the illusion, preferably with strong means based on ethics. Misleading advertising is prohibited but there are clearly large loopholes in areas that require expertise. It is crudely and cynically exploited that not everyone has sufficient competence to stand up to the message. It is sad that available knowledge is not valued highly. Politicians get more power; industries steer the wallet in their direction for increased activity; researchers want projects.

Influence has become more important than information. That is the philosophy and strategy we are facing. We have simply reached a stage in development where the illusion does not break even, though the knowledge is there. This is because, among other things, knowledge is not easily accessible.

There is no shortage of big words. Another established illusory concept in the energy area worth mentioning is the "hydrogen society". It was already put forward for approx. 40 years ago, but since hydrogen did not make any progress for a long time, it was moderated into the "hydrogen economy". "Hydrogen society" creates associations that the whole society will switch to hydrogen and that hydrogen will contribute as part of the solution. Here, it is actually the EU Commission that has taken the lead in creating this illusion. Are there any special interests behind this? With simple facts and logic, we "killed" this illusion in Chap. 3.6 with realistic figures on energy consumption.

A little earlier in the chapter, we mentioned the word "greenwashing". It is, after all, a description of one type of illusion-building in areas that are closely connected to climate and environment. And at the same time, an attempt to establish a new illusion. It is often the oil and gas industry that is most accused of greenwashing. But, in reality, it is what springs from the term "zero emissions" that is the basis for the real big illusion. It is all around us because it works! The connection between increased power demand and emissions is countered by one word, "zero emissions". We must have more zero emissions.

It is the only solution. The oil and gas industry is really only using the renewables gang's illusion of zero emissions from electric power to electrify its platforms. They use the already-established illusion to their advantage.

The same applies to electrolytically produced, so-called green hydrogen. The oil and gas companies have also started to "adopt" it in their communications. All these "technologies" have already been greenwashed by the correct side, who have used paint remover to remove all the black paint. This is a process with very low energy efficiency, around 30%. You don't see that mentioned anywhere.

8.5. Examples of Illusions and the Comfortable Life in the Bubbles

Lies are sometimes nice to have. Just by a little simple free interpretation of the realities and perhaps a little concealment, the world can look much simpler. Advertising uses this consciously and it works best when it does not have to be filtered through consciousness. Politicians use this all the time, perhaps especially in election campaigns, often in the form of slogans, without any arguments. And the most important thing of all: It is repeated many, many times. Then we have a so-called cumulative lie which is very difficult to get rid of. We have created an illusion. In this chapter, we will look a little more at examples of this.

It is easy to create illusions within politics and social life in general. Former President Mr D. Trump was (still is for the same reason) a star example of a politician who deliberately built his power on creating illusions. He brought many very loyal followers with him into the bubble and they are still there. But he went so far that he was seen through by the other more down-to-earth half of the Americans. He almost succeeded! He may even succeed in 2024, largely based on the use of illusions.

Nowadays, a professional group has emerged that calls itself an influencers. These are people who, for payment, preferably good payment, advertise whatever the person who pays them wants—professional liars. There are also large professional agencies that take care of the impact for an ever so small penny, which is big enough for the agency to make a good living on it.

Why is the word "influencer" not negatively charged? The entire advertising industry is designed to plant thoughts and artificial needs in our heads, and even worse are opinions and perceptions.

That is a far more dubious "business" and we are in it every day without noticing it. Today, we have got influence companies.

A lie repeated often eventually becomes a "truth". A "truth" created in that way is an illusion at its very best. Such lies or claims are very handsome sometimes. Imagine, for example, that you are a minister or something like that, who has the task of reducing the country's CO_2 emissions by, for example, 50% over a period of 10 years. It is a difficult task because in your country, there are a lot of cars and boats and planes and everything, and all of this emits CO_2 because they use fossil fuel engines. So, what is the solution?

Of course, we have to electrify. And Norway has a lot of close to emission-free power, and if there is too little, the only thing to do is import from the EU. Norway will not be charged if the EU is so stupid that they still use coal power. The EU has decided that. Besides, the climate quotas will arrange it so that total emissions decrease anyway. This is no problem.

Have you noticed that this influence, the methods and the messages used, have moved more and more into the "world of ethics"? Conscious use of ethics means that they should penetrate as deeply as possible into our souls. Into the very uncritical "I" or "you" where our values are located. It is terribly strong and difficult to defend against. It is demanded that you "can't help it". In that way, the influencers have become far greedier over the years and they want us to feel ashamed if we don't go along.

Today, many claim that they "save the world"; we would like to believe the entire electrification gang and many politicians. You can be labelled as one and the other if you try to argue against "zero emissions", because then you are suddenly arguing against the whole illusion that has been built around electrification, climate, save the world, can't help it. You become a "doubtful one".

Look at the Norwegian plan for climate policy: "Climate Cure 2030". It does not contain a CO_2 account based on pluses and minuses. There are really only minuses. In financial accounting for both companies and individuals, it is a criminal offence to continue like this, isn't it? It is called fraud in the financial world. But, in politics, it is perhaps permissible to be tactical or cunning, or perhaps it is a bit like the purpose justifies the means. If CO_2 is so important for the policy being pursued, the figures should of course be as correct as possible. How does "Climate Cure 2030" achieve this? Yes, they say like most: "Electric power is zero emission energy!"

Today's politicians have put aside the terms "brainwashing" and "propaganda" because they don't do such things, do they? That's what other people do. That's why it has become okay to "influence" and "affect". There is a razor-thin line between these concepts. It is pure brainwashing and propaganda going on around us in the field of electrification.

We think a quote from Voltaire fits well as a conclusion to this chapter: *Illusions are the first of all pleasures.*

8.6. The Diagnosis that Fails to Change the Illusion

Overconsumption is among the top causes of high CO_2 emissions. However, there is probably a little lack of real will in the system to define what is in the category of overconsumption because all consumption is good for "business". It will be up to each individual. No doubt about it, and it's also nice to feel good, so it's easy to leave that problem alone. Politicians also have to be "popular" all the time. There is little time between each election. But unnecessary consumption is to a large extent part of "the big ugly wolf pack" and the underlying cause of unnecessarily high CO_2 emissions. If overconsumption is reduced, energy use is also reduced.

Today, we are actually very good facilitators for more future overconsumption. This means that we provide more nourishment to the very cause of increases in CO_2 emissions. It's a bit unfortunate, to put it mildly.

Reduced energy use, on the other hand, is good for everything, climate and environment included. Is anyone doubting it? And, in addition, it is primarily the Last-power, coal power, that is reduced. Reduced overconsumption would have had a major effect on CO_2 emissions and would have been extremely good for the climate. If an understanding of "overconsumption" becomes the focus, one will also understand that increased energy demand for increased consumption and growth, which illusions now promote as the solution, only leads to increased emissions and is less good for the climate.

Then we are into transport, oil platforms, data centres, cryptocurrency mining, etc. There are elements of increased consumption across the board. You could say that much of this actually is in the category of overconsumption. Do we need it all, here in Norway, where we are already among those at the highest consumption peak? Everything made of metal and concrete must be replaced with more metal and concrete, often long before it is natural time for replacement. Power must be pumped in for more of this. The "will-not-understand-or-do-anything-with-this-movement" lives well with today's illusions and will not break that spiral.

All politics and economics are based on growth. Then a claim to the contrary is difficult to deal with politically. However, there is perhaps too little focus on whether the growth is of real use for something or not. In many cases, the only benefit is that someone makes money from it. It is an accepted rationale today.

It must become more popular to convey common sense again. "Back to basics", or wasn't it in the so-called Enlightenment epoch that people came to the realisation that common sense is not so stupid?

Perhaps climate is really only important in a rhetorical context, as a correct facade. An illusion is being built up that electrified consumption is good for the climate; the more of it, the better. It builds completely irresponsible attitudes. What we are trying to convey in this book is that we must rather take it upon ourselves that anything that increases the use of power also increases global CO_2 emissions much more than what we possibly save by replacing fossil solutions. The question is not whether we should electrify, but when it makes sense to do so.

We should have a parallel to the expression "creating before consumption", understood in the sense that we must not electrify until we have abolished coal power. The correct dosage is important in medical science, otherwise, you can kill the patient. The order is important. As long as we are in phase 1, where coal power is the Last-power, we must put limits to electrification. When coal power is out of the system, we are freer. We show that in Chapter 4, which deals with time perspectives. The climate organisations partially fail the understand these connections. They do not understand that electrification must wait until the prerequisites are present.

They put climate first, and want to electrify now, and thus the emissions increase. That's where we are today. Electric cars, electrification of oil platforms, cryptocurrency, and data centres are well into the heat. They "surf" very well and comfortably on the prevailing climate correctness. The day environmental organisations put all their emphasis on "overconsumption" and "environment", we will more back on track. The "economic law", that everything must increase, is to a large extent guilty of our climate crises. Rather, we must transfer jobs to something that reduces CO_2 emissions (Energy efficiency, production of low-emission energy [read 4GNP], etc.).

The large unnecessary consumption is the underlying cause. It is a fairly obvious analysis if you include a bit of common-sense thinking. But then you have to probably go back in time 300 years, to the Enlightenment. 'It's over,' said Roy.

8.7. Technologists May be Useful

After the war, Europe was rebuilt. Without good technologists who knew their stuff, it would not have been possible. The "oil and gas adventure" was realised. It was a real adventure. You could blame the technologists for that or give them credit for it.

When we think about climate, one might wonder how big a role technologists play in the design of the most important premises of our time. To understand an energy system, you need technologists. To understand the consequences of the system for emissions, you need technologists. But when society wants answers today, they go to economists. Then you get quotas, carbon taxes, and other creative measures, including electrification, which they believe is zero emissions. But unfortunately, this does not result in reduced emissions. It is about managing the cash flows, which is all well and good in many contexts. But when it backfires, it's all a bit sad.

Everything suggests that the role of technologists should be restored, so to speak. At some point in history, this failed.

8.8. The Most Dangerous Illusion?

This one is dangerous because it is not considered by most to be an illusion, and it is certainly not intended as an illusion by its creators; it was even adopted by virtually all UN member states on 12 December 2015: the climate quotas.

Apparently, these take the form of clear rules that guarantee reduced emissions. Most people take this for granted. These rules are good to fall back on when all other arguments fail. "The fox has many exits!"

However, in the climate quota rules, there is a small print. And there, the whole house of cards collapses. The small print means that what looks like a sure guarantee for emission reductions becomes, yes, precisely, an illusion.

But we will not write more about it here: This is dealt with in Chapter 7.

8.9. How Much do the Politicians Really Understand?

We don't think that politicians are stupid but we can say that politics can be stupid. The thinking happens via programs and politicians are more concerned with using illusions and artificial truths for their purposes than breaking down crazy illusions. Illusions are in a way in the politicians' toolbox because they do not see themselves as victims of illusions, and far too much is about what happens at the next election.

However, we must be careful not to lump everyone together. Perhaps there can sometimes be difficult situations that force them to words and actions that give this impression. Or when they actually understand something but which, for other important reasons, they cannot say because it, for example, goes against national interests.

A small example follows. In the EU, all countries, including Norway, report how much reduction of CO_2 emissions they would commit to by 2030. The Minister for Climate and Environment followed up on Norway's magnificent image and gave a little extra: a 55% cut in emissions by 2030. Then and there, they did not think about how it should be done. It's just electrification! It was just to use the redemptive word.

We know that this is very difficult to achieve; at least if there is to be a real reduction and not just a transfer of emissions from Norway to one or more EU countries. To find out how this was going to happen, we inserted hidden microphones here and there so that we could find out how the brilliant climate and environment minister intended to achieve this. Or possibly we were just reading what was said and written between the lines in the past and coming months and years. This survey was so secret that unfortunately, we cannot document whether this happened before or after the last election. But it doesn't really make a difference. At least here is the solution:

The loyal and Ambitious State Secretary (ASS) knocked on the door at the Ministry of Climate and Environment (MC&E): 'Case manager XX says that a 50-page note has been received from a doctor in chemistry and a technical physicist who claims that it is not wise to electrify until coal power in the EU is phased out. They claim that since all other power is used to the maximum, it is coal power that will increase when the use of electric power increases. What are we going to do about this? After all, we have planned a lot of electrifications and that will greatly increase the use of electricity.'

After a very short pause for thought, MC&E replied: 'But the EU has made rules which say that we should only think about what Norway releases. So if CO_2 emissions increase in EU countries that have not managed to phase out their coal-fired power plants, that is not our problem.'

Then MC&E actually thought a little more and added: 'This is, therefore, very simple, it is just a matter of making sure that we replace all fossil-fuel cars with electric cars by 2030, electrify all ferries, all Norwegian ships and planes, and all oil platforms; so suddenly, the problem is solved. If it's a pinch, we can also demand that everyone throw out the wood stoves, brick up their fireplaces, and install heat pumps instead. And until then, there is probably no problem electrifying the planes as well.'

'Yes, heat pumps were a good idea, it even reduces global CO_2 emissions!' ASS answered, who had actually read something both about heat pumps and about electricity, which leads to increased global CO_2 emissions.

'But of course, we have to convince the people that this is what we have to do, so we have to name all these zero-emission cars, zero-emission ferries, zero-emission ships, and so on,' answered MC&E. 'If we repeat this often enough, it will eventually become completely true.' Both MC&E and ASS had learned at political school that it is important to find good positive slogans that are repeated as often as possible. And here, the politicians are in line with science because this is also confirmed by psychological research. So-called cumulative lies that have been allowed to build up over time are almost impossible to combat.

ASS, who had also read a bit about airplanes, cautiously hinted that airplanes would perhaps be a little too heavy due to all the batteries. 'But the EU says that there should be a major investment in hydrogen,' he added.

'Great, then it will be a zero-emission aircraft too,' concluded MC&E. 'Furthermore, it is absolutely certain that Norway's CO_2 emissions will be reduced if almost all transport is electrified. And that is all we have promised will happen. It is not our problem that someone claims that there will be greater CO_2 emissions in countries that produce coal power if we use more electricity. The EU has decided that. We are just loyal to the system. And this memo, just reply that we have noted their opinion, but do not mention the EU,' said MC&E when he ended this important meeting.

This was easier than we thought, both MC&E and ASS thought, *now we were saved because we have read about these difficult cases. And then, it is a bit lucky that we have the EU on our side.*

But one can sometimes wonder, do any of the politicians really believe in "zero emission", and that electrification reduces emissions anyway, or are they just very good actors? In any case, "zero emission" has established itself well and is difficult to get rid of. Many have become an algorithm that plays off the same sentences every time they get the chance. However, if they know that the emissions are not going down as much as they say, but do not mention it because they also know that this is the only way Norway can get its CO_2 emissions approved, then we are on the slightly less honourable side of the matter.

In agreement with the demands of the illusion, one just has to electrify. They then take the chance of being exposed as stupid, rather than being exposed as crooks. And it is always possible to blame others, as exemplified above.

8.10. Media and Illusions

We are not very happy with newspapers and other media. No, we usually call them "Main Stream Media" (MSM) because that is how most Norwegian media behave. It lies in the fact that the media is just passing on the so-called prevailing thoughts, "correct" perceptions, and engaging in conscious and unconscious influence in the prevailing direction. Illusions are created, maintained and reinforced. In a way, MSM is the system's and industry's mouthpiece. There are major contradictions between MSM and critical thinking which should have been a more prevailing ideal.

The media have mostly made themselves subjective and have established terribly narrow corridors of opinion in many areas. You know this sense of "correctness" makes other perfectly legitimate opinions leprous and unacceptable. Look at *Teknisk Ukeblad* (TU, a Norwegian trade magazine especially for engineers), they tend to celebrate everything that is electric and will clearly be a driving force for as much electrification as possible. TU, which should be fact-oriented, should focus more on the whole "story" and be a little more curious about what is behind the facades.

Other newspapers write uncritically about topics that should be elucidated in a far more thorough way in order to better understand the consequences. What appears in print or on the screen is actually often in the category of crude marketing for particular industries and political areas such as electrification and CO_2 emissions. It is possible to wonder if they are sometimes bought and paid for so that they do not dare to write critically about those who advertise in the media. It is not the time of facts, it is the time of illusions! 'Could be the time of invoices,' says Roy.

If you offer a slightly complicated line of reasoning, not to mention a mathematical formula, to a newspaper, then the debate editors will shout and scream that many people will not understand this. Where do public debates end up if it is to be a prerequisite that everyone must understand everything? Or have the sales figures become so important that the newspapers do not dare to include material that many will not understand? 'No one can understand everything,' says Roy.

The MSM is, by nature, based on simple claims so that complicated, important and necessary debates for a well-functioning democracy can hardly occur. Perhaps the newspapers could play a more important and larger role in democracy if they allowed complicated debates at a high level, even if that excludes many of the readers. What happens to democracy without this? Yes, you get today's politicians. Important knowledge is missed! But as long as the country surfs safely and soundly on a cushion of oil money no matter how things are done, who cares?

Where has the curiosity and the ability to raise the questions necessary to develop society further, with an interaction of common sense and scientific understanding where it is natural, gone? The basis for that has probably already crumbled. No one thinks: "This speaks for" and "this speaks against" anymore. The ability to double vision is impaired!

(Double vision means: The ability to simultaneously see a matter from at least two sides, both from the left side and the right side, the tragic and the comic, the serious and the ridiculous in the phenomena of human life, established by the Norwegian author and poet Aasmund Olavsson Vinje about 150 years ago.)

How will we be able to come through with new insights of importance to challenge and balance established thoughts and opinions? Uncritical thinking is not known to bring much good. Then surprises can happen. The future begins now and is electric, isn't it? There are no other truths in the area of energy. Has double vision died? Then the alarm bells in the newsrooms should ring so loudly that it leads to changes. But it doesn't seem like this is possible today. 'Critical journalism does not exist in the climate and energy field,' says Roy.

We believe that one reason why the MSM has arisen may be because the newspapers have become more "moral", that they feel that they must support the important issues in society such as, e.g., view of the climate. It becomes an "ethical" impact. The problem is that they do not have the competence to assess the matters professionally and scientifically. Also, they do not have enough money to set up competent specialist committees to assess difficult cases. We have proposed to set up a competent committee to assess the questions we have raised in this book both to the press and politicians, but we have never received a response.

The media often convey "the correct" MSM stories, and this leads to the same people often being contacted several times; these people often get easy access to the media afterwards. A good illusion-building effect. It can probably vary a little whether it is common sense, morals or money, that is the problem. It is a well-known fact that it is expensive to be poor, especially in terms of brain cells. This most likely also applies on the media front. Perhaps improving the newspaper's finances will contribute to a better democracy.

If Watergate had happened in Norway today, a newspaper would not have raised so much as a finger. We can say that because we see that the scandalous climate treatment in Norway and the EU is much more serious than the poor Watergate scandal in the USA.

Summary Chapter 8

- We have doodled a bit about what illusions are and how they arise and are maintained.
- In today's information society, we now live surrounded by illusions and deliberately tailored information that pushes us in certain directions from all sides. In this society of manipulation, illusions are deliberately created for "someone's" benefit. It's in the time!
- We have pointed to some important illusions that are of great value to many social actors riding the electrification wave. We have exemplified greenwashing. It could certainly have been developed further.
- The illusion builders and those who prevent knowledge from penetrating are mentioned. We think we have managed to point out that it is illusions that are the great problem. The illusions create a mental fog that is difficult to move.
- Associations and symbolism composed in conscious connections stand in the way. "The bend", said Ibsen.

- Profession loses much of its importance when social psychology overrides it. It is easy to become a hostage caught in these "correct" currents.
- Sometimes "correct" currents occur. People can live in different "realities" depending on what they are influenced by, and what they are receptive to, and what they benefit from.
- Why does new knowledge not change these grand illusions? Yes, it is because existential "values" are "ethics" and we are used to establish them. Deep down in the soul—in the very centre of values—"truths" and guidelines for what is experienced as "right or wrong" were planted. The latter largely trumps knowledge.
- Knowledge does not affect "values" of the deep kind! The trap is closed! Only if we know what we don't know, then can we move forward.
- Those who know how to exploit social psychology have a means of power that one should be careful with. And "zero emissions" is a powerful expression that should be stopped abused. That is a fact!
- Mainstream media (MSM) mostly advocate the "correct" stories (often spreading illusional attitudes and misleading information) based on simple claims, such as unsubstantiated zero emissions. Complicated messages, which are sometimes necessary, which will provide other types of answers, the MSM smoothly steers clear of.

9. Basic Conclusions

1. Now, from a climate-relevant macro-scale perspective:

Last-power is the only power type that can vary with consumption. This is coal power because all other powers are fully used. When power is scarce, this situation will remain until coal power is faced out and we enter phase 2.

2. From this, it follows that dedication of low-emission power for special purpose is just an illusion because the amount of Last-power will vary independent of who uses power for what.
3. We have proved that the relation between an electrified and a fossil process in phase 1 equals: [5d] $CO_2\_electrified/CO_2\_fossil = R(CO_2\_fossile\_electrified) * E\_eff\_fossil/E\_eff\_electrified$ For most cases, this is close to 2:

In phase 1, electrification normally doubles the global CO_2 emission.

4. Due to the need to have Infill-power for the unstable wind and sun power: Total power = Stable Power + 2*unstable power => point 5:
5. Because of point 4, we should stop the development of wind and sun-power and use all available recourses for developing 4GNP (Stable, free of CO_2 low risk).
6. 4GNP should be implemented on a large scale as soon as mass production has matured.
7. Until mass production of 4GNP is ready, the use of power should be minimised. All excess power should be consistently used to minimise coal power.

8. Use of hydrogen as an energy carrier should be forgotten until well into phase 3, i.e., after also NG as Last-power has been phased out. Hydrogen still needs surplus power to be a rational alternative.
9. Due to its importance as a fertiliser, ammonia needs to be produced all the time. It should be based on production from gas because that uses less power than produced by electrolysis.
10. Production of e-fuel should wait until late phase 3, the extent depending upon the power supply.
11. We have, throughout the whole book, written about consequences from a time perspective. We would now, at the very end of this book, like to emphasise the seriousness: If we continue as today, we have no chance of getting close to any of the political emission goals, neither for 2030 nor for 2050. And not only that, the emissions will for long periods of time increase instead of decrease. The physical and chemical laws do not listen to wishful thinking without a basis in reality.

References

1. Summary *https://netpower.com*

2. *https://snl.no/kull*

3. *https://www.nrel.gov/docs/fy99osti/25119.pdf*

4. *https://ww2.arb.ca.gov/sites/default/files/classic/fuels/lcfs/lcfs_meetings/12132016wang.pdf*

5. *https://www.mckinsey.com/~/media/mckinsey/dotcom/client_service/epng/pdfs/transformation_of_europes_power_system.ashx*

6. *https://www.dropbox.com/scl/fi/yzm574d7mkyuohb8hccex/ElectrificationMemo5E.pdf?rlkey=k98luqumr855f2osbairscz72&dl=0*

7. *https://www.dropbox.com/s/w2k0z980msiiqm4/AppendixD.pdf?dl=0*

8. *https://www.dropbox.com/scl/fi/yzm574d7mkyuohb8hccex/ElectrificationMemo5E.pdf?rlkey=k98luqumr855f2osbairscz72&e=1&dl=0*

9. *https://www.dropbox.com/s/35uy2jm0v7unbae/AppendixC2.pdf?dl=0*

10. *https://www.dropbox.com/s/7ws8k2taj9t3cbr/AppenddixA.pdf?dl=0*

11. *https://netpower.com*

12. *https://www.euractiv.com/section/eet/news/scientists-warn-against-global-warming-effect-of-hydrogen-leaks/*

13. S. Giddey, S.P.S. Badwal, A. Kulkarni: Review of electrochemical ammonia production technologies and materials.

14. *https://www.statista.com/statistics/1065865/ammonia-production- capacity-globally/*

15. *https://royalsociety.org/-/media/policy/projects/green-ammonia/green-ammonia-policy-briefing.pdf*

16. *https://www.sciencedirect.com/science/article/pii/S2666955223000205?via =ihub*

17. *https://www.irena.org/-/media/Files/IRENA/Agency/Publication/2022/May/%20IRENA_Innovation_Outlook_Ammonia_2022.pdf*

18. *https://netpower.com/technology/*

19. specifications
https://www.dropbox.com/s/8ejhyqbbje4w258/NET-Power-Performance-Data.pdf?dl=0

20. Carbon capture technologies: A review on technology readiness level. Hesamedin Hekmatmehr et.al

21. *https://www.miljodirektoratet.no/globalassets/publikasjoner/m1420/m1420.pdf*

22. *https://www.unep.org/resources/emissions-gap-report-2023*

23. *https://www.statista.com/statistics/276629/global-co2-emissions/*

24. *https://www.shell.com/business-customers/catalysts-technologies/licensed-technologies/emissions-standards/tail-gas-treatment-unit/cansolv-co2.html?utm_term=carbon%2520capture%2520systems&utm_campaign=Carbon+Capture+Storage&utm_source=adwords&utm_medium=ppc&hsa%2520_acc=2377408393&hsa_cam=19307585722&hsa_grp=143244881486&hsa_ad=641920583212&hsa%2520_src=g&hsa_tgt=kwd-*

1200854581414&hsa_kw=carbon%2520capture%2520systems&hsa_mt=p&hsa_net=adwords&hsa_ver=3&gad_source=1

25. https://ccsnorway.com/capture-hafslund-celsio/

26. https://www.regjeringen.no/contentassets/943cb244091d4b2fb3782f395d69b05b/en-gb/pdfs/stm201920200033000engpdfs.pdf

27. https://en.wikipedia.org/wiki/Direct_air_capture

28. https://www.bbc.com/news/science-environment-60312633.amp

29. https://en.wikipedia.org/wiki/Generation_IV_reactor

30. https://energiforsk.se/media/27045/folder-fourth-generation-nuclear-power.pdf

31. https://world-nuclear.org/information-library/current-and-future-generation/molten-salt-reactors

32. https://en.wikipedia.org/wiki/Small_modular_reactor

33. https://aris.iaea.org/Publications/SMR_booklet_2022.pdf

34. https://www.world-nuclear-news.org/Articles/China-s-demonstration-HTR-PM-reaches-full-power

35. https://www.nextbigfuture.com/2022/08/chinas-2-megawatt-molten-salt-thorium-nuclear-reactor-has-start-up-approval.html

36. National CO2 taxes *https://taxfoundation.org/carbon-taxes-in-europe-2021/*

37. EU proposes world's first carbon border tax for some imports | Reuters

38. https://www.dropbox.com/s/7ws8k2taj9t3cbr/AppenddixA.pdf?dl=0

39. https://www.statista.com/statistics/1322214/carbon-prices-european-union-emission-trading-scheme/